I0786292

Working with Transgender and Gender Expansive Clients
Student Edition

A Foundational Guide for Therapists

By

Traci W. Lowenthal, PsyD

Working with Transgender and Gender Expansive Clients
Student Edition: A Foundational Guide for Therapists
by Traci W. Lowenthal, PsyD
Licensed Clinical Psychologist
Copyright © 2018 Traci W. Lowenthal,
https://www.creativeinsightscounseling.com

All rights reserved.
ISBN 9781721144624

You may not copy, duplicate, or distribute this material electronically or physically to use with clients or other self-interests unless you have paid for the book directly through CreateSpace, Creative Insights Counseling at www.creativeinsightscounseling.com, or have received written permission from the author. If you have paid for this material, you may not forward electronically or physically to other professionals, use in professional presentations, or otherwise distribute without written permission from the author.

First edition published in the United States by Traci W. Lowenthal, PsyD

Cover design by Joaquin Gonzalez Dorao

For more information and other queries, contact
drtraci@creativeinsightscounseling.com.

Table of Contents

Dedication

This book is dedicated to professionals and clinicians everywhere who strive to grow in their knowledge of individuals who identify in diverse ways with regard to their gender and sexuality. The desire to learn is not something that is present in everyone, even in the mental health profession. Thank you for your continual search for information to understand and to support others, especially marginalized groups such as these.

I also dedicate this book to my many clients over the last 13 years. I have had the sincere privilege of working over the years with you who have shared your stories and lives with me. In seeking help, each of you has shared your life experience and helped me grow as a person and a professional. I will be forever grateful for the experience of learning alongside and from each of you. My greatest professional gift is watching as you have become your true selves. It is almost as if each of you contains a dimmer switch, placed on low (or off completely) when you first arrived; throughout your hard work and evolution, your switch gradually and beautifully becomes brighter. You have become your own beacon and sometimes a beacon for others. You certainly bring a light into my life.

Letter to Reader

Dear Reader:

I would like to begin our time together with an expression of gratitude for you. Without you, this book and the goals associated with it would not be possible.

For you to have chosen this book, you must have noticed something. Perhaps it was a client mentioning something with which you were unfamiliar. It may have been that you or a family member experienced something related to gender or sexuality. Some readers may be students or parents hoping to understand how a therapist might be useful to them or someone they love. The shared experience of all these perspectives in an important state of being: curiosity or a desire and willingness to engage in the acquisition of new information, likely in your already very busy life.

My strongest hope is that you will read these pages and come away with even more curiosity; that you might be motivated to continue learning about the beauty, depth, and complexity of gender and sexuality, and how each impacts and is impacted by the society in which we live.

Thank you for being willing to read this book, and for your efforts in learning more. Transgender and gender expansive people are still incredibly underserved in the provision of mental health. Curious, motivated practitioners are so needed and important. Though this book wasn't initially written for parents, teachers, and others – I know that those folks may still come to read these pages. Thank you, as well, for doing your part to learn more. As Brian Herbert says: "The capacity to learn is a gift; the ability to learn is a skill; the willingness to learn is a choice."[1]

Thank you for choosing to learn.

Warmly,

Traci
2018

---

[1] (Herbert and Anderson, 2001).

Foreword by Dara Hoffman-Fox, LPC

Thanks to the magic of the internet I was able to dig up the first conversation between myself and Traci Lowenthal, PhD:

October 14, 2014

Hello Dr. Lowenthal,

I was curious as to the name of the Facebook group you mentioned on the WPATH listserv? Am very interesting in joining - was actually considering starting one up, thinking there wasn't one in existence, but am happy to hear you've done so!

Best wishes,

Dara Hoffman-Fox, LPC

At that point in my career I was feeling the typical isolation that can result from being a mental health counselor in private practice, in particular one who specializes in working with gender questioning, transgender, and nonbinary clients. Sure, I had found meaning and purpose through the 2013 launch of my "Conversations with a Gender Therapist" website[2] and Facebook page,[3] followed by my YouTube channel[4] in 2014. I was also connecting locally with a few

---

[2] http://darahoffmanfox.com/
[3] https://www.facebook.com/darahoffmanfoxlpc/
[4] https://www.youtube.com/user/darahoffmanfox

colleagues, all of who were very trans-friendly and hungry for training and resources around serving this population.

But something was missing, which is why Traci's post in the WPATH (World Professional Association for Transgender Health) listserv called out to me. I like to think that, on some level, I must have known this three-and-a-half-year-old email exchange would result in me not only gaining a community of likeminded therapists[5] who share in my passion for serving the trans population, but also a colleague and friend for life.

By 2015 Traci had written a guest blog post for my website,[6] followed by me recruiting her as a beta reader for my 2016 publication, *You and Your Gender Identity: A Guide to Discovery*.[7] Traci was one of my biggest cheerleaders during that period of my life, providing me with invaluable support and encouragement as I slogged through the trenches of creating a book from the ground up.

It should come as no surprise that I was delighted when Traci asked me to write the foreword to *Working with Transgender and Gender Expansive Clients: A Foundational Guide for Therapists*. Besides the sweet synchronicity of coming full circle with each other on our book writing journeys, it has allowed us to collaborate on something that we passionately agree on:

---

[5] https://www.facebook.com/groups/LGBTQIATRANSAFFIRMING/
[6] http://darahoffmanfox.com/dr-traci-lowenthal/
[7] http://discoveryourgenderidentity.com/

There is an imperative need for more trans-aware therapists. Consequently, there is a need to increase the amount of education and training available to those therapists who are willing to step up to the challenge.

It's no coincidence that both Traci and I dedicated our books to the awe-inspiring clients we have encountered over the span of our careers. Having worked with the trans population for a little over ten years now (a few shy of Traci's thirteen), I resonate deeply with what Traci shares in the introduction to this guide when she says, "My greatest professional gift is watching as you have become your true selves."

Traci knows that, especially as mental health practitioners, we have precious little time to devote towards continuing education. Therefore, when we chose to spend time and money on doing so, we must choose wisely. *Working with Transgender and Gender Expansive Clients: A Foundational Guide for Therapists* enables a therapist to do just that.

In this book, Traci covers many questions that cross the mind of a therapist, while doing so in a way that is both succinct and thorough. One could devote a couple of hours towards absorbing the material in this guide and confidently walk away more competent than when they first picked it up.

Additionally, once you become familiar with this guide, you can regularly turn to it as a go-to resource. Creating an affirming office space, the steps of identify formation, what it means to transition, guidance around letter writing, noteworthy terminology... This guide can be used to jog your memory on these and many other topics. From there, you can decide if you have what you need or if further research would prove to be useful.

I also appreciate Traci's conversational approach to teaching these elements of working with gender questioning, transgender, and nonbinary clients. She even offers up examples of when she recognizes, in retrospect, that she was mistaken about a thing or two and how she turned this around into a learning moment (goodness knows I've had mine as well!). This will hopefully reassure you that the goal is not perfection, but a willingness to be humble and accountable when mistakes are made.

Traci is also honest about complicated aspects of working with these individuals (such as requirements around letter writing) that bring up conflict within her. Again, what a comfort to know you are not alone when these challenges come up for you as well.

One of the most essential components of Traci's guide is the "Check-In Time." When working with gender questioning, transgender, and nonbinary clients it is especially important for you to frequently pause and ask yourself questions about your pre-conceived beliefs, privilege, discomforts, and blind spots. By doing so you will expose things which may be difficult to face at first, but ultimately will make you a better therapist.

Traci also hits upon a point that cannot be reiterated enough: this book is only the beginning of your education. Attending trainings, gathering more knowledge and awareness, self-reflecting, and seeking out consultation are all crucial "next steps" for a therapist to take in order to become truly skilled in working with this population.

Traci and I both agree that although we are known authorities in our fields, we are constantly learning right along beside you. The language, theory, and intricacies of what it means to be trans is evolving on a daily basis. This can be both exciting and overwhelming for those of us working in the mental health field. Staying connected with your fellow LGBTQIA-affirmative peers (such as through Traci's LGBQIA and Trans Affirmative Therapists Facebook group[8]) is one of the easiest and most fulfilling ways to stay on top of the most current conversations around these topics.

As a mental health practitioner, you have made the decision to invest your time and energy into reading this information-packed guide. By taking this step to increase your competency in working with gender questioning, transgender, and nonbinary clients, you too can experience the gratification of being an instrumental part of these individuals' journeys.

Dara Hoffman-Fox, LPC
They/them/theirs
Colorado Springs, Colorado
2018

---

[8] https://www.facebook.com/creativeinsightscounseling

Introduction

Welcome to this introductory text on working with transgender and gender expansive people in clinical work! I am thrilled that you have chosen to purchase this book and am honored to serve as a guide to as you begin this journey toward enhanced cultural sensitivity! I am truly grateful that you have decided to make this book a part of your library and to use it to support more people, more fully and in more culturally sensitive ways. This book is a beginning – an opportunity to *begin* to create cultural knowledge and sensitivity and *begin* to understand the nuanced identities of LGBTQIA individuals. As professionals, we know that it is incumbent upon us to pursue proper training and supervision with regard to working with new populations. We know that we cannot read a single book (even this one!) and declare ourselves ready and capable of doing solid therapeutic work with gender expansive individuals.

A colleague of mine, James Guay, LMFT,[9] prefers the term "cultural sensitivity" over "cultural competency."[10] "Cultural competency" implies the idea that we somehow "arrive" at competency and therefore, the implication is that we know all there is

---

[9] NOTE: I recommend James Guay's website at http://www.livingmorefully.com.
[10] (Guay, 2016).

to know on a topic. Within the world of psychotherapy, I do not believe there is any real way to "arrive." Instead, I believe we are on a continual journey. For me (and I hope for you), this is a lifelong expedition, wherein we gather knowledge to assist our clients and ourselves along the way.

Therefore, I would like you to think of this book in this way: this book does not provide you with all you need to know in order to be a culturally-sensitive therapist with gender expansive people. It does however begin to lay a foundation from which you will be able to build upon your cultural sensitivity. Think of this book as a beginning step on your path toward working with this population. My sincere hope is that this book leaves you wanting more – that you use this book as scaffolding toward the gathering of more information and that it will inspire you to seek out trainings and consultation with other well-established professionals in your quest for clinical and personal growth (resources are included in the last chapter).

I am excited that you too will begin to see the beauty, uniqueness, courage, and resiliency present in these expansive communities. I hope that you will work hard to go beyond being an LGBTQIA-friendly therapist to being a therapist who is affirming and knowledgeable of members of this community. (Don't worry – I'll explain the difference a bit later!)

Language and Terminology

As mental health providers, some of our most important tools are our ability to communicate and to understand what others are communicating to us. People communicate through their language and voice, their eyes, their body language, clothing, and many other parts of their outward appearance. It makes sense then, that if we speak only Spanish, we cannot effectively provide competent therapy to someone who speaks only Chinese. In some ways, there is a culture of language within the communities of transgender and gender expansive people: terms, labels, and identities specific to this group of people. If we are without knowledge of the many unique and diverse ways in which LGBTQIA individuals identify, we are at risk for offending, for misunderstanding, and for providing treatment that is ineffective and potentially harmful. Without the use of a shared language, we are left without the ability to communicate effectively with our clients, and they with us. It is for these reasons that we must begin with common language and common terminology.

We must understand the varied ways folks self-identify as well as the ways that people have been *labeled* in negative ways. We must continually seek out this knowledge too, because as people evolve, develop, and change, so do the words and terms that are available to them for self-identification. Old, previously-offensive words are taken and turned into empowering terms; new, nuanced terms are born and shared. It is our duty and privilege to learn and use them.

Definitions

A great example of a word previously used to pathologize and degrade, that is now a term used and even embraced by many, is the word "queer." During the 1970s, "queer" was possibly the worst thing you could call someone. For many folks, however, "queer" represents their gender identity, sexual orientation, or both. For some, "queer" is a political term used to create conversations about liberating individuals and communities from heterosexist or cisnormative narratives. "Queer" is a powerful term – but it is not a term that everyone is comfortable with. My recommendation with this (and with any of the terms listed here) is that clinicians' mirror their client's language and ask them how they identify. Having a blank line on your intake form for "Gender and Sexual Orientation" is a great way to demonstrate understanding for the unique ways our clients identify. If you are unsure, kindly and gently check in with your client.

It is also important to understand that language is constantly evolving. What was acceptable a year ago may no longer be. Therefore, it is important to be steadfast in the commitment to remain aware, as well as to find colleagues and resources that will support your continual quest for information. James Guay, LMFT reminds us, "Terms are crucial and terms are meaningless."[11] What I interpret this to mean is that while knowing these terms is crucial, they are meaningless without the individual explanation that

---

[11] (Guay, 2016).

only our clients can provide to us. I advise that we never assume the definition of a term. Therefore, if two clients say they are trans, it can mean very different things. I always check in with my clients, but never rely upon them to educate me with regard to anything other than their own lived experiences. In other words, I find it most beneficial in my practice to do my homework and to vow to keep doing it! This allows me to honor my work with these diverse individuals with efforts that extend beyond the clinical space.

Following are a list of terms I find crucial in my current practice:

- **Affirming**

  Demonstrating support and compassion for individuals identifying as gender expansive or sexually diverse. As an affirming therapist, this means that I work to be more than just "open" or "friendly" when I work with LGBTQIA individuals. It means I use my knowledge, skill, and training to work hard to create a safe space and experience that goes beyond mere tolerance. Personally and professionally, I really dislike the term "tolerance." I *tolerate* unpleasant things like traffic and insects – I don't believe we should use such a term in relation to people, especially our clients.

- **Binary**

  Binary refers to the system of gender most people

have been socialized to understand. A binary ("bi" meaning "two") system proposes there are only two gender identities: male and female. Many individuals feel that the binary is much too restrictive and that gender occurs on a continuum or a spectrum.

- **Biological Sex**
A person's organs, genitals, hormones, and chromosomes. It is what is assigned to us at birth (or through ultrasound in utero), based on a cursory examination of our genitalia. Biological sex is assumed to coincide with gender identity; for many people, it does not.

- **Bisexual**
A term referring to sexual orientation, indicating attraction to both male and female identified people. (Sometimes shortened as "bi.")

- **Cisgender**
When a person's gender identity is in alignment with their sex assigned at birth. (For example, someone who was assigned male at birth and feels their gender identity is male.)

- **Coming Out**
The act of sharing one's gender identity and/or sexual orientation. Coming out is often thought of

as a singular event, when in fact it is a lifelong
process. Every time someone changes jobs,
moves, or makes new friends--the question of
when, how, and if they share their identity is
present.

- **Gay**
A term referencing sexual orientation; refers to
men that are attracted to men or women who are
attracted to women.

- **Gender Expansive**
A term to describe gender in more than a binary
way; that is to say, more than traditionally male
and traditionally female. A gender expansive
person is able to expand upon their gender and
gender expression in a way that both beyond the
binary traditionalism and is comfortable for them
as individuals. A person may step outside
traditional gender identities of male or female and
may self-identify in ways that incorporate both
aspects of femininity and masculinity or may skew
these ideas completely.

- **Gender Expression**
The way in which someone expresses gender
outwardly. Gender expression does not necessarily
align with gender identity. Society dictates many
ways in which gender is expressed. Clothing,

jewelry, makeup, hair length, and nail length are some ways a person may choose (or may feel compelled to choose, for reasons of safety) to express gender. Gender expression is also present in vocal expression, body language, and movement.

- **Genderfluid**
Someone whose expression or identity is fluid and can change and shift from female to male, or male to female. In this way, gender can be experienced as a spectrum.

- **Gender Identity**
A person's internal sense of self with regard to their gender. It is how someone identifies with regard to their gender. It is separate from sexual orientation and gender expression. Everyone has a gender identity!

- **Gender Non-Conforming**
When a person's gender expression or identity is seen as incongruent with what society deems appropriate for that particular gender. For instance, a person who uses gender neutral pronouns such as "they" and dresses in an androgynous way may be someone who identifies as gender non-conforming (a gender non-conforming person may or may not identify as

transgender). Many people may be gender non-conforming in some ways, but not necessarily identify as being transgender.

- **Gender Neutral**
Can be used to refer to language (for example, the pronoun "they" can be said to be gender neutral), spaces, and items. For instance, a black hairbrush could be said to be gender neutral, but a pink or blue brush would likely be seen in gendered ways. (Don't even get me started on pink and blue!)

- **Homosexual**
A sexual orientation term that has been used to pathologize men who are attracted to men. Also, this is a clinical term that should be used carefully, and only if the client uses it to self-identify.

- **Intersex**
A variety of conditions that involve a person's biological sex (chromosomes and organs) and/or their external genitalia. One example is someone who was been born with ambiguous genitalia. Another example would be if someone's external genitalia resembles a typical male, but internal organs are more typical of a female. "Intersex" is a term that has evolved and some find offensive. Another emerging term is "Differences in Sexual

Development."

- **Lesbian**

  A sexual orientation term indicating that a woman is attracted to women. Some women do not feel comfortable with this term. Many of my younger female-identified clients who are attracted to females use "gay" or "queer" rather than "lesbian." In contrast, many of my clients over 40 use the term "lesbian" to identify themselves.

- **LGBTQIA2S**

  Lesbian; Gay; Bisexual; Transgender; Queer or Questioning; Intersex; Agender, Asexual, or Ally. The *2S* refers to "Two-Spirit."[12] This acronym can vary depending on who is discussing it. I have heard it said that some people don't believe "Ally" should be included because Allies aren't "technically" part of the community itself, but rather are folks who support those within the community. Further, some believe it's confusing to have transgender present in an acronym designed to indicate sexual orientations (as "transgender" refers to gender identity, NOT sexual orientation); many people also use LGBT or GLBT. Furthermore, QUILT BAG is also a useful acronym, which stands

---

[12] NOTE: "Two-Spirit" refers specifically to a term that is culturally-significant to some Native Americans and indigenous people.

for: Queer, Undecided, Intersex, Lesbian, Transgender, Bisexual, Agender, Asexual, and Gay).

- **Masculine of Center**

  A term describing gender identity created by B. Cole of the Brown Boi Project[13] that recognizes the expansiveness of identity for queer or lesbian women who identify more with masculinity.

Non-Binary

Most people think of gender as *either/or*, a binary,[14] as in either male or female. For many people who do not feel their gender is accurately defined as male or female, there are many terms in use to describe their gender identity. The term **non-binary** is one of the most common ways to express the idea of gender as more expansive and less reductionistic than just male or female. Some other terms are *agender*, *bi-gender,* and *genderqueer.* None of these terms mean exactly the same thing, but each speaks to the idea and feeling of gender being something that is not solely male or female.

- **Pansexual**

  A sexual orientation term indicating attraction to

---

[13] (Brown Boi Project, 2010).

[14] NOTE: The term *binary* typically means that something has two parts or two components.

anyone of any gender or sex.

- **Polysexual**
  A sexual orientation term indicating attraction to multiple genders. Polysexuality is said to include those who identify as pansexual and bisexual.

- **Sex Assigned at Birth**
  What we are assigned (typically male or female) based on a visual inspection of genitalia. Often, the third word ever spoken about humans relates to sex: "It's a [boy or girl]!" In some ways, we are also assigned an expected gender identity at birth.

- **Sexual Orientation**
  Who we are attracted to emotionally, physically, and spiritually can indicate our sexual orientation. Sexual orientation is a separate construct from gender identity and should not be conflated. If someone is gay, bi, poly, or queer (or any other orientation), it says *NOTHING* about their gender identity. Likewise, if someone is trans, assume nothing about their sexual orientation. There is no way to discern someone's sexual orientation unless they share it with you. (Similarly, be aware that sexual behavior also does not necessarily reflect a person's orientation.)

- **Transgender**

A person whose sex assigned at birth or biological sex is not congruent with their gender identity. "Transgender" is often used as an umbrella term (meaning, many identities are covered by this term). For many folks, an umbrella term can feel inadequate. It is important to avoid labeling someone as transgender unless they advise you to, or if they use the term to identify themselves. (Important note: It is not considered acceptable to use or say the word, "transgendered." Placing an "-ed" at the end provides the idea that something happened to cause a particular gender identity. In the same way that we wouldn't use the word "colored," when referring to people of color, we shouldn't use the word "transgendered.")

- **Transition**

Transition will be different for each person experiencing it. For some, transition involves medical care such as hormones, electrolysis, and/or surgeries. Each transition is different, and none is more authentic than another. Whether or not a person undergoes any medical procedures, such procedures do not determine if they are transgender or impact their level of trans-ness. Therefore, it is important to honor each individual's right to self-determine what constitutes transition for *them*.

- **Trans Feminine**
  A term describing gender identity, which indicates a transgender person who was assigned male-at-birth but identifies more fully with femininity than masculinity.

- **Trans Man**
  A man who was assigned female at birth but whose gender identity is that of a man.

- **Trans Masculine**
  A gender identity term; indicates a transgender person who was assigned female-at-birth but identifies more fully with masculinity rather than femininity.

- **Trans Woman**
  A woman who was assigned male at birth, but whose gender identity is that of a woman.

Identities and Expression: Visual Explanations

YouTunes

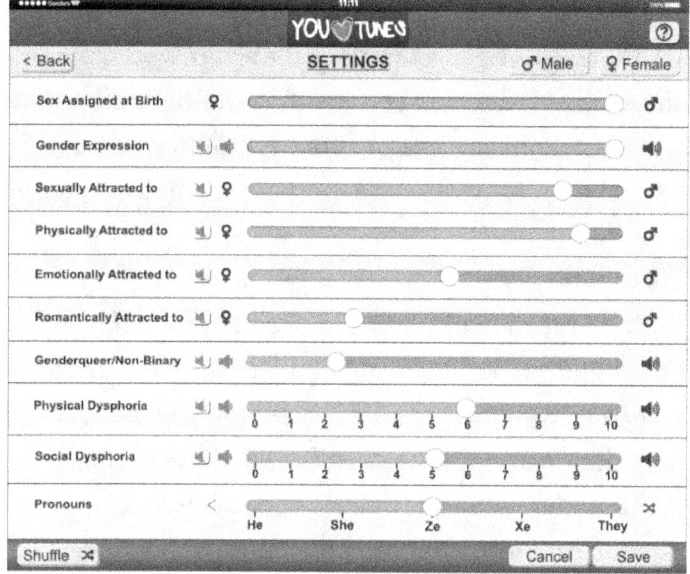

© Traci Lowenthal, 2017

The previous image can serve as a guide for therapists — a way to visualize and understand the many layers of identity that can present related to gender and sexuality. This tablet image is an example of how much variation can be present from person to person. Imagine for a moment that YOU were going to adjust these sliders for your own identity. What might you adjust from the image above? Would you mute any of the options? Do you, perhaps, sometimes wish to shuffle it all? Or some? How would you assist with a client who did? What questions might you ask? Another way to explore this image for yourself is to understand the image might change from day to day or week to week for clients, depending on where they are in their own journey of self-reflection. Perhaps you have never considered the variability that is available for yourself or others. If that's the case — take some time and consider all the ways these layers are present and important to you. After you've had some time to reflect, take what you've learned about yourself and notice any bias that might come up for you with clients. Knowing where our growth edges and counter transference points lie is so critical for our work.

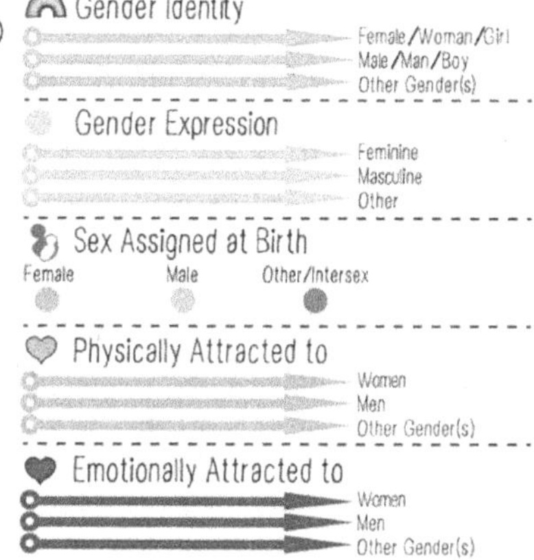

The Gender Unicorn
Graphic by:
TSER
Gender Identity
Female/Woman/Girl
Male/Man/Boy
Other Gender(s)
Gender Expression
Feminine
Masculine
Other
Sex Assigned at Birth
Female
Male
Other/Intersex
Physically Attracted to
Women
Men
Other Gender(s)
Emotionally Attracted to
Women
Men
Other Gender(s)

To learn more, go to:
www.transstudent.org/gender

Design by Landyn Pan and Anna Moore

This graphic is also a wonderful way to explore gender and sexuality with clients (and ourselves!). Super simple and colorful – this is a great tool to understand many components of identity. I imagine that with this image as well, each open circle can slide up and down the line to demonstrate complex variations that may exist from one person to another. There are many other depictions available online. My best advice is to find the image that speaks to you and use that with clients. The more something appeals to you, the more likely you are to feel comfortable using it. An important reminder is to discuss what appeals to our clients as well. They may bring in an image that works best. This is great because it helps us understand their exploration and also lets us gain exposure to new and different tools our clients share with us!

A Discussion of Privilege and Intersectionality

Privilege

The concept of privilege is a complex one. Privilege can be defined as the receipt of opportunities and benefits that a person did not earn through their own action or behavior, but that they benefit from on a regular basis.

These unearned benefits can be given to individuals based on aspects of identity such as race, ethnicity, socioeconomic status, sexuality, and gender identity. The awareness of privilege is also something that frequently causes discomfort and a sense of defensiveness. I personally have experienced this discomfort and will likely again. It is a sign of learning! Please understand that the knowledge of privilege is something powerful. This knowledge can create opportunity, growth, and space for advocacy and activism.

I recall my first awareness of my privilege. I was in my doctoral program at the University of La Verne in a Multicultural Counseling class. One day in class, we began to discuss white privilege. I honestly remember feeling sick to my stomach. The idea that I had access to experiences that other people do not have, solely because of the random experience of being born white, caused many emotions.

My primary emotion was defensiveness. I wanted

to stand up and say, "But you don't know me! I grew up in an economically-disadvantaged home, raised by a single mother…" I felt like I had overcome many struggles in my life! I was ready to offer proof that I didn't have membership in the Privileged Club. I was wrong. After considerable reflection, more conversation, guidance, and reading; it became clear to me that I do, in fact, have an immense amount of privilege. This privilege has many layers – my whiteness, my cis-ness, and my sexual orientation, just to name a few.

How does this privilege play out in my life? A few examples: I am always perceived in a way that is consistent with my gender identity. I do not have to worry about whether someone will use my correct pronouns. I do not worry about being the victim of harassment or murder due to my gender identity or sexual orientation. My driver's license is consistent with how I present in the world. The fact that I never have to think about these issues is privilege. (Imagine the risk and discomfort associated with being asked to show identification. Your identification may have a feminine name and photograph but the gender is listed as male.) When thinking about such commonplace circumstances in life as presenting official paperwork that does not match a person's personal gender identification, it can be easy to see that those people who do not share privilege are often marginalized by it, causing numerous opportunities for pain, exclusion, and discrimination.

For most of us, it is much easier to identify when and how we have been impacted by oppression, rather than when and how we have not.

This experience of privilege doesn't mean that I didn't work hard in my life to achieve or obtain my current situation, but it demonstrates how privilege may have contributed to that achievement or attainment.

Acknowledging privilege does not mean that a person's life is automatically easy, but it may be easier than the lives of others because of the presence of privilege. Make sense? In other words, my life hasn't always been easy, but it's likely been *much easier* than if I were a person of color, a queer person, or a combination of unique identities. Privilege comes in many forms. There is white privilege, male privilege, cisgender privilege, heterosexual privilege, and socioeconomic privilege. What others ways do you recognize privilege? What privileges might you hold?

Check-In Time:

For some, taking some time to write their thoughts and feelings down can bring awareness and clarity. It might also be a wonderful opportunity to speak to a trusted colleague or your own therapist about how privilege has or has not impacted you. As you begin to explore the idea of privilege, how are you feeling? (Please check the Professional Resources section for recommendations on readings related to privilege.) Taking some time away from this conversation is always important if it begins to feel overwhelming. I recommend that you come back to the topic and continue to explore it in your own life, as well as considering it closely in your work with clients. Continue to educate yourself in order to understand more deeply what we ourselves may experience, what our clients, friends, and family members and our fellow humans experience each day.

Consider this an invitation to print or copy this page and write your responses and thoughts regarding privilege here:

____

____

____

____

____

____

____

____

____

____

____

____

____

____

____

____

____

____

Intersectionality

When exploring privilege, we must also be aware of a term known as *intersectionality*. This is a term coined by Kimberlé Crenshaw,[16] who used it to describe the experiences of black women, who experience both sexism and racism. Intersectionality describes the multiple, layered ways someone may experience oppression. For instance, someone may be denied access to medical care, employment, or other opportunities because they are black and a trans woman, or differently-abled and queer.

As providers of mental health support, it is our ethical obligation to understand and explore the presence of privilege in our work as well as in our lives. Understanding the privilege we may carry (or not carry) and hearing the stories of our clients and how their lives have been impacted by the presence of or lack of privilege is paramount to connecting with them on many issues that may be present in our work. Exploring transference and countertransference in our work with clients as it relates to privilege and intersectionality may provide immense opportunities for rich discussions, allowing us to more deeply understand our clients and provide them with the support they need.

Patty Gonzalez, MFT and I hold regular trainings on

---

[16] (Ferguson, 2014).

LGBTQIA issues; during this, we do something we call a privilege walk. A privilege walk invites people to move forward with steps if a particular statement applies to them. One prompt from our privilege walk is: "Take a step forward if this statement applies to you: 'my legal documents match the name I desire to be called.'" This activity leads to a new level of awareness with regard to sexual orientation and gender identity. Privilege walks can be done relating to many different experiences of privilege.

There are many resources available to learn more about this particular activity. For a list of the specific questions we frequently use for privilege walks as it relates to this population, please see the chapter on Professional Resources.

Coming Out

Many people imagine that the process of coming out is an event: a singular, significant moment in a sexually-diverse and/or gender expansive person's life. While there may be a first event of coming out (i.e., coming out for the first time to self or others), coming out is more often a continual process and life-long journey. It's important as clinicians that we support clients in their coming-out process, through having awareness of the potential benefits and risks of doing so. It is also essential that we understand that coming out is not necessarily a goal to achieve, unless the client articulates it as such. Many clients choose to *not* come out. Others will choose to come out in certain spaces, but not in others. I have clients who are out online only, at school only, or at home only.

There is no right way to come out and no blueprint for doing so. When addressing this subject in relations to client, I find it important to monitor my internal agenda, particularly when I was early in the process of developing my sensitivity to these issues. I always wanted to make sure I knew whether I had a desire for my clients to come out or not and to fully explore that feeling. I also made efforts to find colleagues that I trust, particularly those who have experience with this work. There is no shame in having a reaction to the experiences of our clients and their coming-out journey. It's critically important to process these feelings and know them so that you do not allow these feelings to interfere with ethical client care.

Coming out will likely involve many complex feelings for a client (and even for the therapist), such as:

- Fear
- Confusion
- Relief
- Courage
- Empowerment
- Joy
- Freedom
- Pressure

Should the client articulate a desire to share a portion of their identity with others, I often use a solution-focused approach to process the idea of coming out specifically. Here are some questions that I have found useful to pose to my clients as they contemplate a possible coming-out:

- What would the ideal circumstance look like?
- What are you hoping will change in your life after coming out?
- What will be better?
- What might be worse?
- What reactions are you hoping for?

- What reactions are you afraid may occur?

With these questions and the conversations that come from posing them, I have found it helpful to allow my clients to explore all the possible scenarios of coming out.

A Special Note about Youth Coming Out:

For youth especially, creating safety plans around financial support and housing can be crucial. Many young people are kicked out and denied financial support merely because they are gender expansive and/or sexually diverse. Having a solid plan in place is a very important and supportive step to create with your client. Even if financial support and housing are not of concern, emotional safety is also important to discuss. What kinds of emotional safety plans can you help to create with your client? What kind of coping strategies may be necessary to have in their toolbox?

Some of my clients come out to family and friends and are frustrated by how slowly these people manage or adjust to the news. While validating the client every step of the way, I also try to create space for the fact that the client often has been considering this information for years, and the family will also likely need some time to process and learn. This idea is not meant to ever excuse inappropriate or abusive behavior by family but can sometimes remind clients that we may need to be a little patient while others grow and learn. Being prepared with resources to share with family/friends is also a good step for therapists to take. Having resources available on our websites is also important. Often, our clients are placed in the role of educator after coming out. Assisting families to get support and education elsewhere can be a wonderful adjunctive opportunity for therapists to support their client.

Coming out can have many benefits! A client may be able to experience the world with less anxiety and cultivate more emotionally intimate relationships. Our clients may be able to participate (or participate more fully) in LGBTQIA communities where they may benefit from deep connections and shared experiences. Some clients may become role models for others and become more involved in social justice. There are, however, no requirements after coming out! I have had many clients who don't wish to become involved with the LGBTQIA community and this is of course, perfectly acceptable. Allowing our clients to

> determine the path that works best, during their coming out journey and beyond is one our great privileges as mental health providers.

Important note: For many clients, we are the only person they are out to. Honor that space and recognize the trust that requires. Remember this in every conversation, consultation, or other clinical work you do on behalf of or in support of your client. For instance, I work with college students and sometimes will be in contact with campus services around accommodations and such related to academics. A client's coming-out to me would likely have no bearing on any conversation with a dean or other administrator regarding academic accommodation. This is likely true in conferring with psychiatrists and other professionals. If you believe sharing a client's sexual orientation or gender identity is necessary for an appropriate referral or consultation – *always* get specific permission to share this information from your client.

Additional important note, about resources: Be cognizant of resources we share with clients and how they could potentially be "outed" by someone accidentally (or intentionally). Talk about online forums and the need to be aware of who may be able to see the client in those spaces. For instance, if you recommend a Facebook group – let the client know that while some groups are secret, it may still be possible for them to be discovered and to safeguard against that through the use of unique online identities or profiles.

Please recognize that for many individuals, coming out is a truly terrifying event. Honor their willingness to share with you. Thank them for their trust in you. Recognize the privilege of learning such a sacred, important part of who they are in the world. In contrast, for some clients, making a big deal out of their disclosure is actually not positive. Be thoughtful in your responses, and remember the privilege we have as therapists, as well as the responsibility.

Clinical Concerns

Curious about what issues LGBTQIA individuals will bring into therapy? I invite you to check in with yourself as you begin this section. What do you *imagine* clients who identify in these ways will present? Take a moment to jot down these hypotheses. Perhaps you imagined discrimination and rejection during coming out. Or perhaps you find yourself concerned with your clients' relationships? Anxiety? Disorders related to eating? Health concerns? Job stress? Parenting?

Check-In Time

Consider this an invitation to print or copy this page and write your responses and thoughts regarding therapy in relation to LGBTIQ individuals here:

____

____

____

____

____

____

____

____

____

____

____

____

____

____

____

Regardless of what came to mind for you, it's important to remember that our LGBTQIA clients may present with concerns related to gender and sexual identity, but many will not.

In the infancy of my clinical practicum training, I reviewed intake packages for new clients and see that someone identified as gay or transgender; I would imagine that these layers of their identity would form the basis for seeking care. Let me tell you: I was incredibly wrong. Thankfully, I had thoughtful, gentle supervision that allowed me the opportunity to notice these potentially damaging heteronormative and cis-sexist beliefs and examine their origins. While being aware of someone's multiple identities is paramount, utilizing a hyper focus on one component of their identity is rarely useful; such a focus can even be harmful. If we attribute a person's struggles in life to being gay and/or trans (or being a person of color, a person of different abilities, or any other identifiers that make people unique), it's dismissive of *all* of who they are.

Clinical Concerns: The Impact of the *DSM*

The *Diagnostic & Statistical Manual (DSM)* has a difficult history in relation to the queer and transgender communities. It wasn't until 1973 that the diagnosis of "Homosexuality" was removed.[17] While this was a step forward, the term was replaced with "Sexual Orientation Disturbance." In 1980, the diagnosis was changed further to Ego-Dystonic Homosexuality. Finally, in 1986, sexual orientation was removed as a diagnosis completely.

Sometimes it is jarring to consider: less than 30 years, ago people were being diagnosed as mentally ill because they identified as gay. When I consider the folks I know who are gay or queer, chances are many of them could have been and were diagnosed with an illness just because of who they found themselves attracted to. While this isn't a proud moment in mental health professional history, the movement toward change and the continual efforts of many passionate activists created these huge shifts in systemic perspectives.

With its latest edition, the *DSM* also creates concerns regarding gender identity. The first diagnostic label, Gender Identity Disorder (GID), was introduced into the *DSM-III* in 1980. The *DSM-III-R* re-categorized GID into the diagnosis of gender

---

[17] (LGBT Issues Committee, 2011).

identity disorder into three types: "Transsexualism," "Non-Transsexualism," and "Not Otherwise Specified."[18] The first two were then combined into gender identity disorder in _DSM-IV_. In the most recent, fifth edition, Gender Identity Disorder was replaced with Gender Dysphoria (with qualifiers based on age).

While shifting from labeling people with a mental disorder to identifying an experience of dysphoria is an improvement, it is far from perfect. While many transgender people _do_ experience dysphoria that would meet clinical criteria, many do not. For those that do not however, being diagnosed with Gender Dysphoria may create a path toward medically necessary, sometimes insurance-funded, medical care, should they desire it as a way to experience congruence with their body and gender identity.

Here are the diagnostic criteria as directly quoted from the _DSM-V_:[19]

Gender Incongruence (in Adolescents or Adults)

A. _A marked incongruence between one's experienced/expressed gender and assigned gender, of at least 6 months duration, as manifested by 2 or more of the following indicators:_

---

[18] (American Psychiatric Association, 1987).
[19] (American Psychiatric Association, 2014a). NOTE: Does not include subtypes.

1. *a marked incongruence between one's experienced/expressed gender and primary and/or secondary sex characteristics (or, in young adolescents, the anticipated secondary sex characteristics)*
2. *a strong desire to be rid of one's primary and/or secondary sex characteristics because of a marked incongruence with one's experienced/expressed gender (or, in young adolescents, a desire to prevent the development of the anticipated secondary sex characteristics)*
3. *a strong desire for the primary and/or secondary sex characteristics of the other gender*
4. *a strong desire to be of the other gender (or some alternative gender different from one's assigned gender)*
5. *a strong desire to be treated as the other gender (or some alternative gender different from one's assigned gender)*
6. *a strong conviction that one has the typical feelings and reactions of the other gender (or some alternative gender different from one's assigned gender)*

Subtypes

    With a disorder of sex development

    Without a disorder of sex development

For the adult criteria, we[20] would like to propose on a preliminary basis, the requirement of only two indicators. This is based on a preliminary secondary data analysis of 154 adolescent and adult patients with GID compared to 684 controls.[21] From a 27-item dimensional measure of gender dysphoria, the Gender Identity/Gender Dysphoria Questionnaire for Adolescents and Adults (GIDYQ), we extracted five items that correspond to the proposed A2-A6 indicators (we could not extract a corresponding item for A1). Each item was rated on a 5-point response scale, ranging from Never to Always, with the past 12 months as the time frame. For the current analysis, we coded a symptom as present if the participant endorsed one of the two most extreme response options (frequently or always) and as absent if the participant endorsed one of the three other options (never, rarely, or sometimes). This yielded a true positive rate of 94.2% and a false positive rate of 0.7%. Because the wording of the items on the GIDYQ is not identical to the wording of the proposed indicators,

---

[20] NOTE: *We* here references the American Psychiatric Association.

[21] (Singh et al., 2010).

further validational work will be required during field trials.

Clinical Concerns: Identity Formation

As with many aspects of our human experience, knowledgeable mental health providers have created models from which to understand the development of parts of ourselves. With regard to sexual orientation and gender identity, there are a several models we should be familiar with. My personal view of these models is this: no client traverses any of them in linear ways. Some clients may skip stages, move through, back and forward and back again depending on support, trauma, loss, and other life experiences. I recommend these models as guides for you as a clinician to understand where your client may be. (A big shout out to UNC Charlotte Safe Zone[22] for this succinct provision!)

---

[22] (University of North Carolina at Charlotte, n.d.a).

Homosexuality Identity Model by Dr. Vivienne Cass[23]

In 1979, Dr. Vivienne Cass released a stage model based on her research related to identity development in gay men and lesbian women.[24] Dr. Cass's model was based on her empirical research with predominantly white people of middle to high socioeconomic status in Australia. Though the sample is less than ideal in terms of diversity, it is still a well-recognized model and one that is often taught in higher education. It is a useful guide in many ways but doesn't necessarily embody the experiences of all transgender people or gender expansive people. It should also be noted that, as with many stage models, people do not necessary transition from stage to stage in a linear fashion. People may stay in one stage for a long period of time, or several stages. Possibly they may go from one to another and back again for a time. In my view, the point of a model like this one is to hypothesize how your client may be experiencing their own identity development at any given time. Further, if we see a client who is already at a point of Synthesis (the last stage of this model), it may be useful to

---

[23] NOTE: This model is based on research on mostly white gay men and lesbian women of middle to high socioeconomic status. Additionally, this stage model does not necessarily reflect the process that a bisexual or transgender individual may go through. Ultimately, this stage model may not be applicable to everyone.
[24] (University of North Carolina at Charlotte, n.d.a).

explore their development as a guide to their process. Below are the stages as delineated in the original model, with my thoughts on what a person may experience in each stage:

Stage 1: Identity Awareness

Here the individual is aware that they are "different" from others in some way. They may not understand exactly how, but they may begin to feel separate from others. This experience may lead to confusion and avoidance or denial of these feelings.

Stage 2: Identity Comparison

Individuals in this stage begin to compare themselves to others who they identity as heterosexual. It seems that the major task of this stage is to attempt to align with those who are straight or gain curiosity into whether or not that alignment exists. The idea of "maybe I am gay" begins to emerge.

Stage 3: Identity Tolerance

People begin, in this stage, to tolerate the idea that they may be queer or gay. Individuals also may begin to explore the possibility that they are gay. Additionally, individuals more closely begin to notice other gay people and may begin to interact with others who are perceived to be gay.

Stage 4: Identity Acceptance

During this stage, folks may begin to seek out more information through readings or activities to learn more about gay culture. They begin to identify as being gay and may come out to a few select people. Some may continue to feel unsure about identity.

Stage 5: Identity Pride

People may feel deep sense of pride related to their identity and group, but also may possibly feel disdain or discomfort with majority culture. May avoid interacting in mainstream groups. An "I'm different and proud!" feeling predominates.

Stage 6: Identity Syntheses

A person may experience full acceptance and integration of their identity and previous beliefs and ideas related to being "othered" or "othering" non-gay individuals. In general, I find that clients in this stage accept who they are and feel more at peace with themselves.

Homosexual Lifespan Development Model by Anthony D'Augelli[25]

Anthony D'Augelli developed the next model, the "Homosexual Lifespan Development Model," which he released in 1994. This model, like the previous one indicates that phases are not experienced in a specific order but rather these phases can be experienced in any number of ways or multiple times. (As stated previously, this has also been my experience with the earlier stages of the Cass model.)

D'Augelli posits that the following experiences are part of the developmental trajectory during a gay person's identity development:

- **Exiting a Heterosexual Identity:** Similar to the Cass model wherein an individual develops an awareness that they are not part of the majority and that their identity is different.

- **Developing a Personal LGB Status:** This is identified as a time for an individual to come out to themselves in terms of identifying as a gay, lesbian, or bisexual individual.

---

[25] (University of North Carolina at Charlotte, n.d.b).

- **Claiming an Identity as LGB Offspring:** This is the process of coming out to family members and to close, important individuals.

- **Developing LGB Intimacy Status:** This stage involves exactly what it sounds like: forming intimate relationships with people of the same sex. (I personally would expand this to include gender identity as well).

- **Entering an LGB Community:** This stage involves being open about identity in multiple spaces, and potentially also being active in the LGB community in multiple ways.

Lesbian Identity Development Model by Susan McCarn and Ruth Fassinger[26]

Another development model is the Lesbian Identity Development Model by Susan McCarn and Ruth Fassinger, which was created in 1996. This model examines identity development from both the personal and group perspectives.

Awareness

- The perception of being different from other people. Also, a growing awareness that other gay people exist.

Exploration

- Beginning to investigate the feelings toward other same sex individuals. May or may not include sexual behavior.

Deepening/Commitment

- Internalization of identity as a gay or lesbian individual.

---

[26] (University of North Carolina at Charlotte, n.d.b). See also https://scholarworks.uvm.edu/cgi/viewcontent.cgi?article=1075&context=tvc.

Internalization/Synthesis

- The integration of sexual identity into overall sense of self/identity.

It was thought that a woman could not reach the final integration/synthesis stage without also beginning to explore the group identity connected to sexual orientation. With regard to group identity, Fassinger created four stages:

1. **Awareness:** Understanding that other people exist with different sexual orientations.

2. **Exploration:** Curiosity and exploration of a person's relationship to the gay community.

3. **Commitment:** Committing to the gay/lesbian community, which an awareness of the negative experiences/consequences that may accompany this commitment.

4. **Internalization:** Acceptance of gay identity throughout various contexts in life.

Transgender Emergence Model by Arlene Istar Lev[27]

In 2004, Arlene Istar Lev, LCSW-R, released the Transgender Emergence Model. As with the previous models, this is a stage model that explores how transgender people come to understand their identity. Lev's model provides information about the experiences of an individual, but also what mental health providers should also be aware of in their work. A client seeking care may be at any stage of this model at the time they seek care:

- **Awareness**
  In this initial stage, an individual is aware that they feel different, and may be experiencing distress due to this awareness. Lev identifies the therapeutic task is to normalize the experiences of evolving as a transgender individual.

- **Seeking Information/Reaching Out**
  The second stage is typically with trans/GNC people are seeking information/education and support about being trans; our tasks as healers are to help create connections and provide resources.

---

[27] (University of North Carolina at Charlotte, n.d.b). See also: https://www.amazon.com/Transgender-Emergence-Therapeutic-Guidelines-Gender-Variant/dp/078902117X

- **Disclosure to Significant Others**

  This third stage involves coming out as trans to significant others such as family, friends, and spouses/significant others. Our tasks as therapists involve assisting the client in being integrated into the family systems as their authentic self.

- **Exploration (Identity & Self-Labeling)**

  The fourth stage is when clients explore trans identities. Our role is to aid and support our client in identifying and articulating who they are with regard to their gender identity.

- **Exploration (Transition Issues & Possible Body Modification)**

  The fifth stage involves clients' exploration of options for transition. This can involve identity, presentation, and physical changes. The therapeutic task is to help clients determine and move toward their goals in these areas. It is also likely to involve some advocacy on the part of the therapist.

- **Integration (Acceptance & Post-Transition Issues)**

  In the sixth and final stage, the transgender person is able to integrate their identity. Our role is to support and assist the client with adapting to any transition issues they may be experiencing.

Clinical Concerns: Mental Health and Diagnostic Considerations

Please note I didn't say "comorbid diagnoses." While many clinicians do use the term "comorbid diagnosis" when referring to a gay or trans person, I hope that you will now feel encouraged and empowered to refute this idea. Such terms can sometimes provide a clinician advocate an opportunity to educate someone else.

I hope that you will find a new layer of awareness related to how often folks pathologize someone's sexual or gender identity. These ideas are deeply entrenched in societal norms. However, I hope that you will be able to say it with me: being gay or trans is NOT mental illness.

Diagnoses with regard to gender expansive and sexually expansive individuals obviously vary. Some of the diagnoses I routinely encounter with my clients are anxiety, depression, obsessive-compulsive disorder, and gender dysphoria. I also encounter individuals who struggle with eating concerns, addiction, relationship issues, phase of life problems, sexual assault, and academic or employment struggles. In other words, what transgender and queer individuals present with clinically often mirrors what cisgender and straight people present with.

None of this is, however, intended to minimize the very real struggles that our clients present with. How we explore the mental health concerns our expansive clients present with is more important than attempting to tie diagnostic labels to gender and sexual identities. How anxiety presents in a transgender woman of color will likely look very different than how it might present in a Caucasian, cisgender woman. The coping strategies we help our client develop will also likely be different based on identity, existing coping skills, and support.

One of the things that I say repeatedly to clients, colleagues, and friends is: "Being transgender or queer is **not** the problem. How society often reacts to these identities **is**." While we support our clients in their quest for authenticity and inner contentment, we must also strive toward educating the public. As clinicians, we provide our clients with tools to cope and heal as an intrinsic part of our work. But I cannot stop there. To do so, essentially ensures that these clients' struggles will almost certainly continue. Systemic change and advocacy is something I feel that we as clinicians must attempt to engage in when and where we are able.[28]

Clinical Concerns: Gender Dysphoria

For those clients who are open to it, I encourage them to learn more about mindfulness and how to use it to work through their more difficult gender dysphoric [GD] moments. One of the most useful exercises for GD is to learn to accept the feelings they are having by focusing attention on where that sensation is in their body and breathing into it instead of trying to fight it. This can increase self-compassion, as well as reducing the intensity of the feeling itself.
--Dara Hoffman-Fox, LPC[29]

When using Google to understand the word "dysphoria," a searcher can find many, highly-varied explanations and definitions. As a provider working with gender expansive people, "gender dysphoria" is a term I hear often both from clients, in publications and trainings, and with regard to diagnosis. Though I hear about dysphoria most often in those who are gender expansive, it is important to recognize that *anyone* can experience dysphoria.

---

[29] (Quotation appears courtesy of Dara Hoffman-Fox, LPC).

Dysphoria typically involves a feeling of dissatisfaction or discomfort with some portion of or the entirety of a person's physical, mental, or social self. Gender dysphoria can be related to physical traits like having a penis or breasts or having a particular physical shape. It can be related to the existence of body hair or the absence of it. It can be caused by menstruation, by height, or lack of either. I think of dysphoria as the feeling that arises for folks when their body does not match their internal sense of self. For someone who identifies as female, showering and having to exercise hygiene related to having a penis can create a great deal of dysphoria. I have found that the experience of showering is quite as difficult for many trans-identified folks as is sexual activity for others. One thing that is very important to recognize is some people do not experience any dysphoria at all. If someone doesn't have dysphoria, it doesn't make them any less trans.

I find that questioning my clients about dysphoria needs to be done in a sensitive way. Many clients come to treatment with the understanding that they must present in a specific way, often based on what they have been told or what they have read online. I have had clients state they were having intense dysphoria when our work began. Then, after trust has been established, I find out they have very little or no dysphoria but they were afraid to say so, due to a popular belief that they must have dysphoria to be considered "trans enough" to get a letter or support for medical care.

For many of my clients who do experience it, dysphoria can be managed or minimized in a number of ways. Exploring a client's coping skills is generally my first stop on the journey of assisting in the management of dysphoria. I find that helping a client identify ways that can lessen negative experiences that trigger dysphoria is a good first step for some clients. For instance, this may involve helping a trans masculine person problem-solve and anticipate the dysphoria created by menstruation. I also explore assisting clients in moving away from ineffective or dangerous coping methods. Some such methods may include substance misuse and/or abuse, self-harm behaviors, and avoidance of proper hygiene. For many clients, beginning a medical transition is what begins to ease their dysphoria. This, however, is not always an option, due to finances, insurance, or life situations. Also, not every client wishes to utilize medical intervention as part of transition. Helping clients find healthy ways to cope with dysphoria is something clinicians need to be ready for.

Of course, another early step in managing dysphoria is identifying it. Some people haven't yet been able to put a name to the deep sense of unhappiness they have currently or even have experienced for years. Sharing information with clients about what dysphoria is and how it can present is an effective way to help support their understanding of themselves and their experience.

Self-care is an important tool in the work of lessening dysphoria. Helping our clients create self-care plans they can stick with is important. Self-care can be exercise, music, time with friends and loved ones, pets, time outside, and creativity. Helping the clients we serve to identify and utilize what brings them joy and comfort is one of our roles as therapists. Further, we can help clients identify what may trigger their dysphoria and empower them to create a plan around that.

Clinical Concerns: Family

In my own practice, I find that many clients identifying as queer or trans experience difficulties in family relationships. Over the years, thankfully it seems my clients experience less and less of this, but when it happens, it can create profound pain. Families may choose to completely disengage from a queer relative. Depending on the age of your client, this estrangement can create other difficult experiences such as poverty or homelessness. As previously mentioned, I find that this awareness is especially important when working with clients around issues of coming out. Other family members may pretend nothing is going on and never speak of a person's sexual or gender identity. This can work for some families but can create difficulty – especially if a client feels they have to hide a relationship or important pieces of their lives. Such a lack of open communication can chip away at emotional intimacy within families.

When possible, I work with families; when not possible, I try to provide other kinds of support resources (like books, websites, or support group information). It's important to remind clients that it is not their responsibility to be the educator of all things related to sexual or gender expansiveness. It is okay and healthy to help provide information to parents or other family members and encourage further information acquisition from other places. As a therapist, I support this by having local and web-based resources available to share. I will also meet with family for group consultation sessions (of course, only if my client desires this), as a way to demonstrate support for my client and to share resources.

Clinical Concerns: Discrimination

Many clients will have experience with discrimination. This can be present at their jobs, homes, and daily living. For some, such discrimination can create deep emotional wounds. I have had clients who have lost their jobs or been unable to find a job which was likely related to discriminatory practices. Feelings of shame, distrust, anger, low self-esteem, frustration, hopelessness, and anxiety can all be related to discrimination. As of this writing, in my home state of California, it is illegal to discriminate against someone because of their gender identity or sexual orientation.[30] This is not the case in all states.

In the Professional Resources section, you will find a link to the Transgender Law Center's Equality Map. This can be a helpful resource for therapists and clients to determine what constitutes discrimination in a particular state or town. If it is determined that an event in your client's life was illegal, you may then be able to support your client should they wish to move toward addressing the discrimination outside of your

---

[30] (Bellis, 2016).

office. However, you need to be prepared to honor your client's wishes should they choose not to discuss these issues beyond the therapeutic relationship.

Another important issue to note is that LGBTQIA folks often live with a baseline experience of EXPECTING discrimination and stress. The moment they leave the house (and sometimes within their homes) they wake up KNOWING that they are likely to be harassed, abused, or denied care or services because of their trans identity. Operating from a place of such extreme vigilance on a daily basis takes an emotional and physical toll. For this reason, I find it exceptionally important to be mindful of the environment I create in my office.[31]

---

[31] NOTE: More on this later; see especially the section entitled, "Affirming Office Spaces."

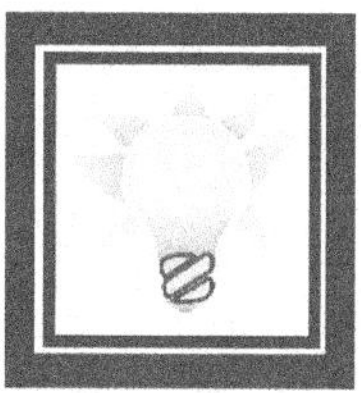

Clinical Concerns: WPATH (World Professional Association of Transgender Health) and ICATH (Informed Consent for Access to Trans Health Care)

Clinics providing medical services to transgender individuals adopt one of several models for care; two of the most prevalently used are: WPATH and ICATH (discussed below). When working with transgender individuals, it is important to be aware of these standards.

World Professional Association of Transgender Health (WPATH) and its Standards of Care (currently in version 7) describe themselves in this way:[32]

WPATH, previously known as Harry Benjamin International Gender Dysphoria Association (HBIGDA) is a 501(c)(3) non-profit, interdisciplinary professional and educational organization devoted to transgender health. Our professional, supporting, and student members engage in

---

[32] (WPATH, n.d.).

clinical and academic research to develop evidence-based medicine and strive to promote a high quality of care for transsexual, transgender, and gender-nonconforming individuals internationally. We are funded primarily through the support of our membership, and through donations and grants sponsored by non-commercial sources.

Mission *to promote evidence-based care, education, research, advocacy, public policy, and respect in transgender health.*

Vision *to bring together diverse professionals dedicated to developing best practices and supportive policies worldwide that promote health, research, education, respect, dignity, and equality for transgender, transsexual, and gender-variant people in all cultural settings.*

Many clinicians find membership in WPATH to be invaluable. As with any large organization, others find it less useful. I encourage you to explore whether WPATH is a membership you would find value in. Regardless of your decision, it's important to be familiar with the current Standards of Care as relates to the care of transgender people. A free, downloadable copy is available, under "Publications" on the WPATH.org website.

The Standards of Care (SOC7) are **guidelines** for working with transgender individuals (not immovable rules or regulations). While I won't restate the entire SOC7 here, it's important to note they recommend a mental health care provider write letters of support for those clients wishing to undergo medically necessary care (see next section for more on this). Many physicians and insurance companies follow these standards of care and will require a client to present a letter (or two, depending on the procedure) from a mental health provider; this letter essentially documents that the person is capable of making the decision to undergo the procedures they are seeking.

There continues to be concern that this requirement pathologizes trans-identified people. To further explain this, consider what would happen if I decided to have a hysterectomy, breast augmentation, or a cosmetic procedure to further feminize my face. As a cisgender woman, I would not be required to see a mental health provider and get a letter; I could just make an appointment for the procedure. I invite you to take some time to consider that. A transgender person who desires a particular surgery is frequently required to provide a letter from a mental health provider. This can be costly, time-consuming, and exhausting. Additionally, in many cases, this letter is required to include a diagnosis in order for the client to access the medical care and/or insurance payment. This is clearly problematic. The problem inherent here is that the person has to receive a diagnosis of a mental illness in order to get the care they require. That diagnosis is often what allows a person to get the medical care they require but it may also be what **prevents** them from getting care. The diagnosis of gender dysphoria is something that is required by *some* insurance companies to get hormones, surgery, or other medically necessary care, and some insurance companies specifically deny coverage for those with that diagnosis.

Another model is known as the Informed Consent for Access to Trans Health Care (ICATH) Model. This model, currently used by only a few practitioners, makes space for the idea that transgender folks are able to make decisions about their care without having to receive mental health care. A person can seek medical care without a letter. This obviously removes barriers to care and creates opportunity for trans folks to access medical care in the same way that cisgender people do every day.

My personal approach is this: if I am able to refer a potential client to an informed consent clinic, I do. In my own circumstances however, the closest informed consent clinic to my office is over an hour away. For some folks, that distance is more of a barrier than coming to me to request a letter. When possible, I have clients work with medical providers that do not require letters, but sadly that is rare.[33]

---

[33] More about letters later, in the section entitled "Letter-Writing and Gate-Keeping."

Transition

Merriam-Webster[34] defines *transition* as:

1 a: passage from one state, stage, subject, or
place to another: change
   b: a movement, development, or evolution from
one form, stage, or style to another
2 a: a musical modulation
   b: a musical passage leading from one section
of a piece to another
3: an abrupt change in energy state or level (as of
an atomic nucleus or a molecule) usually
accompanied by loss or gain of a single quantum
of energy

Interestingly for me, each of these definitions
misses the mark in some way when considering the
word "transition." I experience my clients' transition,
in whatever form they take, as a slowly increasing
beauty; the brightening of an inner light; the growing
of an inner strength. A becoming.

For some, *transition* means an increase in
masculinity or femininity. For others, it's the decrease
of one of these. For others, it is the melding of
different pieces of themselves to form—for possibly
the first time—a cohesive and true sense of self. For

------

many people, transition is more about gender expression than changing; others seek to evolve, change, or adjust their physical self-using medical services, medications, or interventions.

My point here is: THERE IS NO RIGHT WAY TO TRANSITION.

It really bears repeating: THERE IS NO RIGHT WAY TO TRANSITION.

I hear people within and outside the community sometimes say, "I want to go all the way." I also hear folks say, "Well, have they had The Surgery?" But, what "all the way" means is personal. Likewise, what constitutes The Surgery is different for everyone. Some folks do not pursue any type of surgical support, nor do they want to.

My advice is to never assume that you know what your client needs or wants. I find that clients respond best when you listen to what they are looking for and take their lead. If you find that you have an agenda about what any client wants or needs, I strongly recommend that you check in with a colleague and receive consultation and supervision as necessary. An outside perspective can help you grow in your knowledge and understanding, and your clients to move in the direction that is best suited for each of them.

Keeping all this in mind, it's important as providers that we maintain an understanding of the many ways clients can seek to support their own transitions.

There are many activities which clients engage in to feel closer to the best versions of themselves. Listed below are many of the interventions/confirmations clients seek. We are not medical professionals and must not practice outside our scope, but helping clients as they explore, evaluate, and consider different paths IS certainly part of our scope as therapists.

Medical Interventions: Hormone Therapy

Feminizing and Masculinizing Hormones[35]

Hormone therapy is a medical process frequently used by many of my clients, though of course, it is not used by all. Folks who identify as female may wish to utilize feminizing hormone therapy. Those that identity as male may choose masculinizing hormone therapy. Gender non-conforming folks may also seek hormone therapy. For adolescent clients, puberty suppression may be an ideal path.[36] Helping our clients prepare for hormonal therapy is an important step. We too, must understand what is likely to happen in the pursuit of this care.

1. **Education Regarding Options, Including Risks and Benefits**
   Frequently, the goal of my conversations with clients around hormones is to explore their

---

[35] (Deutsch, M. B., MD, MPH, n.d.a).

[36] NOTE: Working with transgender-identified children is out of the scope of this publication. Should you be considering this, be sure to invest time in specialized training.

knowledge of the available medical intervention, as well as any related risks and benefits. We also discuss what the client knows about reversible and non-reversible changes that will occur with regard to any chosen path. Of course, for those of us who are not physicians, medical conversations are out of our scope; but it is often useful for clients to have a safe place to discuss their fears and concerns about a particular treatment, as well as having support in creating questions for their medical provider.

For example: for some, male-pattern baldness is an irreversible side-effect of testosterone therapy.[37] Exploring this potential outcome with our clients can be quite illuminating and helpful as they investigate options. Also, discussing changes that impact sexual activity (if your client is sexually active or desires to be) can also be important as it may affect significant portions of a person's life and relationships with loved ones.

2. **Blood Work**

Blood work will be required for all clients seeking hormone therapy. This helps to establish current levels of hormones and helps doctors determine the correct dosing.

---

[37] (Deutsch, M. B., MD, MPH, n.d.b).

3. **Administration**

   Once the correct dosing (or a starting dose) has been determined, there are many ways for hormones to be administered. These include injections, oral administration, creams, suppositories, pellets, etc. Of course, it is not our role to advise clients on the correct form of administration; however, we can and should help clients troubleshoot the choices, and aid them in being compliant. For example, a client might have a fear of needles, but believes injections to be more effective. In this important support role, clinicians can work with clients in encouraging open conversations with related medical providers; likewise, therapists may also need to helping clients manage related anxiety (in this example, finding coping strategies for needle-related anxiety).

Here is some very basic information regarding hormone therapy. Please see the Professional Resources section for links to more detailed information.

Feminizing Hormones:

Feminizing hormones may take several months before changes are noticed and several years before changes are complete. These changes are not reversible, even if someone stops hormone therapy after a period of time. The time it takes for any or all of these changes varies across individuals.

Some of the **permanent** changes that patients can reasonably expect are:

- changes in breast size (growth of breast tissue),
- changes in the size of testicles (will become smaller and softer).
- individuals utilizing feminizing hormone therapy will likely become infertile; therefore, conversations around fertility can be very useful.[38]

Reversible changes (changes that will most likely reverse, should hormone therapy be stopped) include:

- changes in fat and muscle distribution.
- some trans feminine clients report loss of upper body strength and the development of a more feminine body shape due to changes in fat distribution.
- emotional and mood changes can take place as well (for example, if a client presents with

---

[38] More on this later in the section entitled, "Letter-Writing and Gatekeeping."

significant mood impairment prior to the introduction of hormones, I find it beneficial to discuss with my client how this information can be shared with their medical provider, in a way that manages any changes in mood due to hormones).

- changes in libido and erectile function may also occur for clients using feminizing therapy.

It's important to note that based on levels of testosterone, many clients will also need to take an androgen blocker to lessen the production of testosterone. This is one more support function we clinicians can provide by encouraging our clients to speak to their doctor about the side effects of androgen blockers (and other medications like it).

Masculinizing Hormones:
Changes produced by masculinizing hormones may also take months to become noticeable and years to complete.

Some of the **permanent** changes are:
- a deeper voice,
- increase in body/facial hair and coarseness,
- loss of hair/male pattern baldness, and
- growth of the clitoris/phallus.

Some **reversible** (changes that will most like reverse, should hormones be stopped) changes may include:

- acne,
- increase in energy,
- increase in libido,
- increase is muscle growth/strength,
- changes in fat distribution,
- changes in mood,
- increase in anger or aggression, and
- loss of fertility (NOTE: some clients choose to explore harvesting eggs for later use if they believe they may want biological children in the future).

More about Hormone Therapy and Sexual Behavior

Hormone therapy may affect fertility but is not a reliable source of protection against pregnancy. For clients who have gonads (ovaries or testes), they may also need to explore contraception. This need is, of course, impacted by whether your clients are engaging in penetrative sex. It's important to avoid assuming that clients are engaged in any particular type of sexual activity or that they want to engage in any sexual activity at all. The range of activities that bring people of all genders and sexual orientations pleasure is vast; therapists must be careful to not make heteronormative assumptions about the behaviors our clients engage in. Likewise, we must never use our clients as examples indicative of behaviors engaged in by everyone who identifies in a similar. I strive to remember that each client is the expert in their own life.

When talking about sexual activity, it is a good idea to check your biases again. What reactions do you have as you begin to explore the range of sexual behaviors clients may engage in? How do you feel about talking about fertility, sexuality, and contraception with your clients? These also might be good conversations to explore with a trusted colleague or supervisor.

Interestingly, based only on my direct, anecdotal clinical experience, for some people, hormone therapies seem to improve mental health in general. I cannot necessarily say (again, not being a physician) that this is because my clients taken a positive step toward feeling their most authentic; nor can I assert that the introduction of hormones with trans people provides their brains with something that was missing all along. Perhaps in time, medical research may be able to vindicate this correlation and discover if this is a genuine phenomenon.

Medical Interventions: Surgeries

A NOTE ON TERMINOLOGY: My first recommendation is to abandon the term "sexual reassignment surgery." This is offensive and problematic for many people. A lot of trans identified folks do not feel that they are "reassigning" anything, but rather confirming who they really are. As with other aspects of communication, model the language your client uses. Be curious about the terms they use and be willing to explore with them the terminology they have chosen. Further, continue to listen to the community in general to continue your awareness of how language evolves and changes. My currently preferred term is "gender confirmation surgery," but as with so many other aspects of this subject, I typically follow my client's lead on this. If a client uses "sexual reassignment surgery," I may even say something like, "I noticed you use the term 'sexual reassignment surgery.' Can you share more about what that term means to you? Does it feel true for you?" Being curious can help us understand our clients and perhaps help clients understand themselves a bit more.

An important point: Our role as therapists working with transgender individuals will likely involve writing letters in support of clients obtaining medically necessary interventions such as hormones and surgeries. I personally believe that it is important for us to have at least a basic understanding of what these procedures entail.[39]

A non-exhaustive list of procedures clients may be interested in:

- Hysterectomy:
  Many transmasculine men seek out hysterectomy as part of their transition. Hysterectomy can be combined with other procedures but can also take place separately. Clients may wish to undergo multiple procedures at once, for various reasons.

- Metoidioplasty:
  Metoidioplasty can be an option for folks who do not wish to undergo a phalloplasty. Simply, it involves surgical release of the enlarged clitoris and can also involve urethral

---

[39] More on letter-writing and medical necessity later in the following section, "Letter-Writing and Gate-Keeping."

lengthening. Surgeons work with their unique
patients to determine which procedure will
create the best possible outcome for their
patients. Whether a client wishes to stand
while urinating and have penetrative sex can be
determining factors.

- <u>Orchiectomy</u>:
  Many trans women seek out orchiectomy. This
  procedure is the removal of gonads/testicles;[40]
  however, the phallus is not removed. Some
  trans women choose to retain scrotal skin for
  use in a vaginoplasty (see below) at a later
  time. Sometimes, the orchiectomy takes place
  at the time of the vaginoplasty. Some folks
  prefer to have an orchiectomy done to alleviate
  or lessen the need for androgen blockers (see
  hormone therapy, above).

- <u>Phalloplasty</u>:
  Phalloplasty involves the creation of a phallus
  or penis. There are different types of
  phalloplasty, typically based on the donor skin
  site. Donor skin can be taken from the arm, the
  thigh, or the back. Penile implants can be
  included later, after significant healing has
  taken place. Phalloplasty can be done alone or

---

[40] NOTE: This procedure is not specific to transgender individuals.

alongside other procedures. Again, each client's preferences for penetrative sex, urination, and aesthetics can all be conversations clinicians have with clients.

- Salpingo/Oophorectomy:
Salpingo (removal of fallopian tubes) and oophorectomy (removal of ovaries) are procedures that clients may also request.

- Top Surgery:
My experience has been that most clients who discuss "top surgery" are transmasculine, non-binary, or identify as male. In contrast, my female identified clients usually say, "breast augmentation" or "boob job." For transmasculine folks, "top surgery" refers to a masculinizing chest surgery, involving the surgical removal of breast tissue. There are various ways for this surgery to be done, and helping our clients weigh the method they are interested as well as creating safety around speaking to their surgeon about their options is often an important component of care.

- Vaginectomy:
Essentially, this is the obliteration of the mucosal lining of the vagina and closing of the walls of the vagina using sutures. The

removal/obliteration of the mucosa eliminates secretions. Sometimes this procedure is done with scrotoplasty, testicle implants, and metoidioplasty.

- <u>Vaginoplasty:</u>
  Simply put, this procedure creates a vaginal opening and canal, most often using a penile inversion. An orchiectomy is performed as part of this procedure, if not done previously. The scrotal skin is often then used to create labia and a portion of the glans penis can be utilized to create a clitoris. Talking with our clients about this procedure can range from understanding the actual procedure, searching for and choosing a surgeon, and developing an aftercare plan. With vaginoplasty, after-care is quite involved and includes the time-consuming activity of dilation. Speaking with clients about how to manage these procedures, as well as aftercare, can be of great support.

Sometimes my role in surgical decision can be to sit with clients and look at options online; sometimes, I may be providing links to information. It can also be helping clients connect with and reach out to folks in the community who may have more information. Another important component of our work with clients is helping them to be aware of and plan for

appropriate post-operative care.[41] Being a clinician
with this population necessitates that I also
understand what a client may need to plan for in
regard to post-operative care. My role for any client
contemplating surgical or hormone treatments is not
to frighten clients with extensive lists of potential risks
and complications, but rather, to help them sort
through the information they have and create a plan
that works for them. Assisting in the realistic
expectations of what follows a surgery can be an
essential part of my job.

---

[41] NOTE: Of course, this is true for any surgery and for any client.

Check-In Time

Consider this an invitation to print or copy this page and write your responses and thoughts regarding transition and medical interventions here:

____
____
____
____
____
____
____
____
____
____
____
____
____
____
____

Letter-Writing and Gate-Keeping

NOTE: Before beginning the conversation about letter writing, I want to take a moment to re-state that reading an introductory book like this does not constitute competency or expertise. I do not want, in any to way, to suggest that because someone has read this book that they are now able to go out, begin seeing transgender clients, and writing letters for their medical care. We know as therapists and mental health providers that it is incumbent upon us to seek out proper training and supervision. My intention is that this book serves as an informative first step toward the acquisition of additional information. If you get a call from a transgender client looking for support next week and you've never sought any other support beyond this book, I hope that you will refer that client to a more experienced therapist. If you are not able to refer that client (due to location or other issues), I would hope that you would immediately begin supervision or consultation with an experienced supervisor.

Likewise, this section about letter-writing and gate-keeping is also a foundation of knowledge and not intended anything other than a brief, foundational explanation of letters. If you wish to move toward writing letters, please do so! We need more qualified therapists providing this! But, please do so only after seeking out supervision, consultation, and training.

As mentioned previously, one reason for familiarizing ourselves with the medical procedures some clients may want is because of clinicians are often asked to write letters. As of this writing, I get at least one weekly request for a letter. These requests may come from existing clients or complete strangers. For some, the letter is all they need; for others, therapy is also a path they would like to travel.

In order to understand letter writing, we must of course understand the WPATH Standards of Care and Informed Consent, but when it comes to letter writing, if you were to ask five different therapists how they do it, you would likely get several different responses. Some therapists write letters that are many pages long and detail a client's experience of gender with explicit detail. Others might even include a section about how the client experienced puberty.

Over the years, my own letters have evolved to include much less detail. When a client decides to see me for a letter, I explain that I will be asking them about their knowledge of the procedures or surgeries that they are about to undertake as a way of being able to include in the letter that they are making an informed decision.

I also ask about the following details:

- <u>Gender History</u>

    When asking about gender history, I gently inquire about a person's first awareness of being something other than cisgender. Some folks might confide, "I've always known." Others might say, "Well, I knew something about me was different and I thought I was gay. So, I came out as gay. Then, I realized it was something different. I found the word 'transgender' on the internet and it perfectly described my experience."

    Of course, there will be a range of responses. They are all correct. I never assume that someone is confused if they have only identified as being trans for a short time or that they didn't realize until they were 20. I try to separate myself from the stories and stereotypes so common in modern-day culture. Some individuals will identify knowing that their gender was different than their assigned gender from a very early age; others will not. It does not make anyone less trans if they discover something about themselves later in life.

- <u>Experience of their body</u>

I gently inquire about how the client relates to their body. I use open questioning and never assume. An example is: "Can you tell me a little bit about how you feel about your physical self?" Many people have been taught that trans people hate their bodies. That may or may not be true for any individual person. Some clients experience intense difficulty with seeing or touching their own bodies. Others do not. I have helped clients create coping strategies around showering, but many are fine showering. Almost all of my trans masculine clients have sought out top surgery, but not all. Some transgender women have sought vaginoplasty while in my care; others maintain a phallus and derive sexual pleasure from it. Each client is different and their experience of their body is different, just as with any client. In my letters, I may state, "John Doe experiences intense physical dysphoria and seeks mastectomy as a means of creating more congruence and comfort with their body."

Other letters may not include this type of language.

- <u>Whether the client meets the criteria for Gender Dysphoria in the *DSM-V*/ Diagnosis of Gender Dysphoria</u>[42]

  In essence, the diagnosis of gender dysphoria is meant to indicate distress created by incongruence of gender assigned at birth and experienced gender identity. Here again, are the reprinted criteria for the diagnosis of Gender Dysphoria from the *DSM-V*:

Gender Incongruence (in Adolescents or Adults)
A. *A marked incongruence between one's experienced/expressed gender and assigned gender, of at least 6 months duration, as manifested by 2 or more of the following indicators [subtypes not included here]:*
1. *a marked incongruence between one's experienced/expressed gender and primary and/or secondary sex characteristics (or, in young adolescents, the anticipated secondary sex characteristics)*
2. *a strong desire to be rid of one's primary and/or secondary sex characteristics*

---

[42] (American Psychiatric Association, 2014b).

because of a marked incongruence with one's experienced/expressed gender (or, in young adolescents, a desire to prevent the development of the anticipated secondary sex characteristics)

3. *a strong desire for the primary and/or secondary sex characteristics of the other gender*
4. *a strong desire to be of the other gender (or some alternative gender different from one's assigned gender)*
5. *a strong desire to be treated as the other gender (or some alternative gender different from one's assigned gender)*
6. *a strong conviction that one has the typical feelings and reactions of the other gender (or some alternative gender different from one's assigned gender)*

Some of the language of this diagnosis is problematic for clients. For clients seeking letters, it is nearly always necessary to include a diagnosis of Gender Dysphoria. The physicians often require this, as do many insurance plans that clients utilize. I have a conversation with my clients about this so that they are not surprised or traumatized by seeing something in their letter they weren't expecting.

- <u>Sexual Experiences</u> (depending on the surgery in question)

  Depending on the age of the client, and the procedures they are seeking, I will inquire about sexual experiences. I do not do this because of a preconceived, heteronormative expectation of what sexual behaviors someone should have engaged in prior to receiving their medical care. I do this to explore someone's comfort with their body and to discuss with them how sexual activity and behavior may be impacted (positively or negatively) as a result of their contemplated medical procedures.

  I also explore what clients hope for in relation to their chosen medical interventions and explore realistic hopes and desires. For some clients, sexual activity either is not important or is non-existent in their life, by choice or circumstance. This would never prevent me from writing a letter. I may include something like, "Client shares that they are aware of changes in sexual function that will or may occur as a result of this procedure/intervention."

- <u>Fertility</u> (depending on the surgery or procedure in question)

In discussing fertility with clients, I am particularly careful to pay attention to my own biases and beliefs. I never assume that someone wants to have biological children. There are incalculable ways to create a family, should a client want one. Surrogacy, adoption, and sperm- and egg-donation; the list goes on. This conversation can be especially hard with younger folks. Asking a 19-year-old whether they plan for biological children can feel burdensome. Many folks are already aware (even at young ages) what they want for their future selves. Many of my clients have known, without a doubt from when we met, that they do not want children. Others have been certain they do. Others still are unsure and choose to preserve fertility through egg harvesting or sperm storage. I have had more than one client ask a family member to donate eggs or sperm for the creation of a family that contains a biological link. Each client is unique.

Therefore, I find it helpful to ask questions like: "Can you tell me a bit about what your future family looks like?" and "Who is a part of your future life?" I find it very interesting to listen to the beautiful ways clients share their future visions with me. If someone doesn't mention children, I might say, "I notice your imagined life does not include children. Can you say more about that?"

With this information, my letter than can include a sentence like, "With regard to fertility, Mr. Doe states they may desire children in the future, and plans on adoption as the means of having children." Another example might be: "Jane Doe has considered her fertility options and indicates having no desire for biological children."

- <u>How long the person has been living authentically, in terms of their gender and sexuality</u>

Many physicians wish to know how long a client has lived as their authentic selves. This can be difficult to navigate as old rules required certain amounts of time as living "full time." For some clients, living full time is not possible due to safety, housing, finances, etc. If this applies for a client, I include it in the letter (for example, "Sam Jones has been living authentically as male, at home and at work for three years"). For others, I state, "Client has identified as male for one year." I have never had a doctor request clarification on this. If a doctor did require clarification, I would confirm my information release with my client and offer more information, always checking with my client first.

An additional note about letters:

I experience a lot of personal and professional conflict about writing letters. On one hand, I am honored to support clients by writing letters for them to get what they need. I attempt to do so in a way that makes the process as simple as possible and in as short amount of time as possible. But I also sometimes resent the need for the letter. As stated before because I am cisgender, I could get hormones or breast augmentation when and where I would like to. I do not need a letter to do so. The situation itself is a source of frustration for me on behalf of my clients; but I have learned that my resentment isn't useful to include in the wording unless I am engaged in advocacy.

I discuss with clients what will be in my letter and I often show it to them prior to sending to the requesting physician. I attempt to be as transparent as possible in the process to limit the experience of gate-keeping. I open the dialogue around their experience of having to see me to get the letter. I explain that I am a force for their support and want to help them get what they need. Period. Most of my clients appreciate this transparency and begin to feel safer about the process of seeing a therapist and obtaining the required letter.

Finally, if you're a therapist in California with a client that would be supported by a letter, or if you would like to discuss consulting or training opportunities with me, please reach out!

Health Care Access for Transgender People

As therapists, it is important to know that a large portion of the transgender community lives in poverty. A study published in *The Guardian* in December 2016 shares data gathered from 27,000 respondents.[43] Of those, one-third indicated they lived in poverty. Trans people experience unemployment at significantly higher rates than cisgender people as well; the same *Guardian* article reported unemployment rates in the trans respondents at three times higher than cisgendered respondents. While this is just a snapshot of some of the experiences of transgender people, it brings forth an important point: the lack of healthcare access and finances for large segments of the trans community. When we explore how difficult it is to obtain health care in the first place, and then layer upon it a requirement that a trans person get one or two letters to receive the specific health care they need, it seems clear that making obtaining health care easier for trans folks to receive rather than more difficult and costly is incredibly important. Further,

---

[43] (Lartey, 2016).

many transgender people are denied health care **simply because they are transgender**. Therefore, I see my role is to support our clients in the acquisition of affirming health care, both inside and outside of the clinical setting.

Suicide

Suicide is the second leading cause of death among youth age 10 to 24. For LGBTQIA youth, the rate of attempt is approximately 4 times higher.[44] If a young person comes from a highly rejecting family, those rates are even higher. For transgender individuals, between 40% and 45% report attempting suicide at some point across their lifespan. In other words – as mental health providers we need to be aware our LGBTQIA clients may present to us with higher levels of risk because they identify in this way. **Let me clarify though: this is not _because_ of their identity, but because of how society views and responds to their identity.** These rates are not indicative of pathology present in this community. It is indicative of how much education, advocacy, and support are still needed in the world. It is also evidence of how desperately we as competent mental health providers are needed.

---

[44] (The Trevor Project, n.d.).

Affirming Office Spaces

Whether you are just beginning to work with the LGBTQIA community – or whether you have been working with the community for years – creating a safe, accepting environment in your office is something relatively simple but that has a huge impact on clients. When clients enter our offices, just as many places in their worlds, they will likely begin to assess for safety. They will look for indications that your office is a safe, accepting place.

There are many ways to communicate inclusiveness and acceptance in your office. Here are some opportunities:

Web-Presence: Remember that often, our clients' first experience of us is through our website, online marketing, or social media. Be sure that your site includes language and information supportive to the LGBTQIA community. For instance, if I find a therapist on *Psychology Today* or another similar directory, and they advertise as LGBTQIA-friendly, I will then likely go to their website. If their website has nothing about expansive identities, I will likely not refer to them. Being affirming isn't a marketing tactic; it's a way of being in the world. Of course, it's unethical to state that you're a competent therapist for this community if you aren't. But if you are trained to specialize, be sure to include this on your website! This can be done with specific language, images, book recommendations, and blogs.

Business Cards: Take a look at your business cards. Is there any indication that you work with expansive communities? My business card has a stripe of rainbow colors on the bottom and my tag line is: "Psychology. Affirming. Everyone." When I chose this, I worried about being *too* specific in my marketing, such that folks who are not in the LGBTQIA community would feel they couldn't reach out to me for care. This has not happened. My cards work well for me because for those who are part of the community, there is information that is relevant to them communicating my affirming approach. For folks who are not part of the community, it merely appears to be a colorful business card.

Office Forms: Our forms are another kind of first meeting with a client. Whether you have hard copies of your forms or use a virtual system, be sure that there are many ways a client can identify and many opportunities to describe family structure. I personally love having the field "Gender" followed by a blank line on my own forms. This allows a client to self-identify. I also recommend this for Sexual Orientation and Relationship/Family Structure. It allows clients to share with us and also communicates to them that we are not locked into limited ways of existing in the world. I also invite feedback from clients about forms—including the question, "Did you have any questions or concerns about the paperwork?"—can be simple non-threatening way for clients to share their experiences of our forms.

> My approach with clients, as an EMDR Trained therapist, is to encourage them to do things like adult coloring books and blowing bubbles. One modality of EMDR therapy is to help clients to create and utilize a mental Safe Place.[45]
> --Sonya G. Adams, LCSW, (Clinical Social Worker), LCDC (Licensed Chemical Dependency Counselor)

Office Environment: Our office environment offers multiple ways to communicate that we are affirming therapists. Take a moment to look around your office. What do you notice? What might be apparent to someone who is assessing the room for safety and understanding? Begin there to look at everything with a critical, considerate eye.

---

[45] Quotation appears courtesy of Sonya G. Adams, LCSW, LCDC

For example, what books do you have on your shelves? Do you have any titles that would communicate that you are affirming? For instance, my book shelves have books about anxiety and therapy in general, but also books specific to the LGBTQIA community. I have children's books on the subject, as well as books for adolescents and adults. It's not enough to just put these books on your shelves, though. We need to have read them so that we know if they are appropriate to recommend to clients. I work hard to never share a resource without vetting it first.[46]

Pictures/Artwork: Do you have artwork in your office? Like most therapists, I do have photos in my office that are sans people. If your art has people in it, are they only straight, cisgender people? Are you able to add representations of many kinds of people?

Magazines: What types of magazines are available in your office or waiting room? This is one of the first areas that clients may notice. Do you have magazines that typically depict heterosexual and cisnormative individuals? It might be time to find more inclusive publications!

---

[46] NOTE: I am sometimes asked: does this take lots of extra time? Yes, sometimes it does – but to me, this time commitment is part of being an ethical therapist.

Bathrooms: Do you have gender-neutral bathrooms? For some therapists, this may not be within your control. My office building had gender-segregated bathrooms for a long time, but I shared that information with clients. When they would ask where the restroom was, I would say, "They are down the hall, and I want to warn you that they are not gender neutral. That's something I'm aware of and working on." The bathrooms in my building require numerical codes for entry, so I would then tell the client both codes so they could make a decision on which restroom to use. While the situation isn't ideal, it's a chance to share your awareness with clients about something that could deeply impact them.

Non-Discrimination Policy: A clearly-posted non-discrimination policy can be a great way to indicate to clients that they can feel safe in your office.

Staff: Be sure that *EVERYONE* on your staff is trained in correctly greeting clients on the phone and in person. Rule Number One? Don't assume! If someone phones, do not use terms like "sir" or "ma'am." For many of us, this omission can feel uncomfortable: many of us have been conditioned to believe that doing so is a sign of respect. It takes great effort to unlearn some of what we've been taught about gender! Please make every effort to stop gendering people without allowing them to do so first.

I also recommend that staff not assume what pronouns a person uses. Using a person's correct name is also critically important.

The following pages (available to copy as a reference guide) are an example of how I advise my staff to handle phone calls:

STAFF PHONE GUIDELINES

Staff: "Thank you for calling Creative Insights Counseling. How many I help you?"

Caller with a deeper voice: "Hi. I'd like to make an appointment with Dr. Traci."

Staff: "Perfect. I'll need to gather some information from you first and then we can get you scheduled. What may I call you?"

Caller: "Um. Well, I go by Sarah."

Staff: "Wonderful, Sarah. I'll be sure to note that here. May I also indicate your pronouns?"

Caller: "Yes, please. 'She' and 'her.'"

Staff: "Great! Thank you! Now, to set you up in our system, I apologize, but I will need to have the name that is listed on your insurance card as well. Is 'Sarah' the name on your insurance? Or is there another name? May I have that?"

Caller: "Yes, okay. It's 'Matt Smith.'"

Staff: "Thanks Sarah, I will put that in our records, but I will let Dr. Traci know your name is Sarah."

Now, a call may not always be so clear cut, but this gives you an idea of how to begin navigating calls and inquiries. Also, if I receive an email from a potential client and that person has an email of Robert Smith, I don't typically begin my email with "Hi Robert!" I avoid using a first name until I have clear indicators from the client that this name use is appropriate.

Professional Resources

DISCLAIMER: These links are being provided as a convenience and for informational purposes only; I have found them helpful in my own practice. However, I can bear no responsibility for the accuracy, legality, or content of the external site or for that of subsequent links (aside, of course, from my own website). Contact the external site for answers to questions regarding its content.

This list is by no means exhaustive, but instead, should be considered a beginning from which you may discover many more sources.

Also, please note: At the time of this publication, these links were accurate and live. However, they may no longer be available. Please use your own good sense when looking for updated information, as needed.

Counseling, Education, and Training by State

General

LGBTQ Therapist Resource
http://www.lgbtqtherapistresource.com/

Gender Care: My On-Call Doc
http://genderprogram.myoncalldoc.com/

Gender Sexuality Info/LGBTQ Resource Directory &
Events Calendar
https://gendersexuality.info/

Alaska

Identity Alaska
http://identityalaska.org/resources/

California

Inland Empire Area
Creative Insights Counseling
https://creativeinsightscounseling.com/

Central Counseling Services
http://www.centralcounselingservices.net/

Los Angeles Area
Jen Bailey, MA, PsyD
https://www.psychologytoday.com/us/therapis
ts/jen-bailey-camarillo-ca/264493

BLVD Treatment Centers
https://www.blvdcenters.org/

Heather Brewer, LMFT
http://heatherbrewermft.com/

The Center for Mindful Living
http://www.mindfullivingla.org/offerings/mind
fulness-classes/

Dr. Shannon Chavez
http://drshannonchavez.com/

Dr. Lani Chin
http://www.drlanichin.com/

Mary Kay Cocharo, LMFT
http://www.mkcocharo.com/

Creative Insights Counseling
http://creativeinsightscounseling.com/

Jamie Elvey, MA
http://www.relationshipwellbeing.com/

Gay Therapy LA
http://www.gaytherapyla.com/

Darren Goldstein, LMFT
http://www.darrengoldstein.com/

Ashley Graber, MA, LMFT
http://www.ashleygrabertherapy.com/

Grow UR Potential Therapy Practice
http://www.growurpotential.org/

Yisraela Hayman, LMFT
http://www.yisraelahayman.com/

Michel Horvat, MA, LMFT
http://www.couplestherapistlosangeles.com/

Rashel Keshimiri MS, LMFT
http://www.racheltherapy.com

LGBTQ Affirmative Therapist in O.C.
http://www.therapy4lgbt.com/

Living More Fully
http://livingmorefully.com/

Los Angeles Gender Center
http://www.lagendercenter.com/

New Awakenings Therapy
https://www.newawakeningstherapy.com/

Vessela Papazova, LMFT
http://www.vesselapapazova.com/

Cindy Paxton, PhD, MS, LMFT
http://www.cindypaxtonlmft.com/

Jacqueline Plante, LMFT
http://www.jacquelineplantetherapy.com/

Rena Pollak, LMFT, CGP
http://renapollak.com/

Relationship Therapy LA
http://www.relationshiptherapyla.com/

Dr. Amy Rosenblatt, PsyD
http://www.dramyrosenblatt.com/

Elham Shoa, LCSW
http://www.elhamshoa.com/

Soul Tenders
http://soultenders.com/

St. John's Well Child & Family Center
http://www.wellchild.org/

SVC Therapy Solutions
http://www.scvtherapysolutions.com/

Tell Your Story Therapy
http://www.tellyourstorytherapy.com/

Through the Woods Therapy Center
http://www.throughthewoodstherapy.com/

Transgender and Gender Nonconforming
Affirming Therapy
https://www.gendersupport.com/

Orange County Area
Yasaman Mohtasebi, MD
http://www.prohealthpartners.com/biocards/yasaman.htm

Sunburst Youth Housing Project
http://www.thecentersd.org/programs/youth-services/youth-housing-project.html

Transgender Affirming Therapy in Orange County
http://www.transgenderaffirmingtherapy.com/

Palm Springs Area
Michael's House
http://www.michaelshouse.com/

Riverside Area
Quality Life Group
http://qualitylifegroup.com/

San Diego Area
Dr. Jennifer Bahr
https://resiliencenaturopathic.com/

Metamorphosis Medical Center Transgender Clinic
http://www.metatranshormone.com/

Dr. Stuart Rubenstein
https://www.cpcmg.net/

Trans Family Services
http://transfamilysos.org/

Dr. Abi Weissman
http://www.doctorabi.com/

San Francisco Bay Area
Dr. Erica Anderson
http://www.drericaanderson.net/

East Bay Trans Counseling
http://www.eastbaytranscounseling.org/

The Gender Health Center
http://www.thegenderhealthcenter.org/

Cathy Hanville, LCSW
http://www.cathyhanville.com/

SF Therapy Collective
http://www.sftherapycollective.org/

Adam Zimbardo, MFT
http://www.adamzmft.net/

Sacramento
Jenna Ghazanfari, MS
http://www.folsomhealing.com/

Colorado

Nyle Biondi, MS, LMFT
http://www.nylebiondi.com/

The Bohemian Sanctuary
http://www.thebohemiansanctuary.com/therapist
-referrals/

Gender Identity Center of Colorado
https://giccolorado.org/

Dara Hoffman-Fox, LPC & Gender Therapist
http://darahoffmanfox.com/

Massachusetts

Bethesda
Shawn V. MacDonald, PhD
http://www.macdonaldpsychology.com/

Boston
Fenway Health
http://fenwayhealth.org/care/behavioral-
health/

New Jersey

BN Counseling
http://www.bncounseling.com/

New York

Elijah C. Nealy, PhD, M. Div., LCSW
http://www.genderodyssey.org/blog/go-spotlight-dr-elijah-nealy/

Dr. Kelly Wise
http://kellywise.com/

North Carolina

Asheville
Porchlight Counseling Asheville
http://www.porchlightcounselingasheville.com

Oregon

Oregon Trans Health
https://oregontranshealth.com/

Spectrum Counseling
http://spectrumcounselingpdx.com/

Texas

San Antonio
Faith G. Harpern, PhD, LPC-S, ACS
http://faithgharper.com/

Utah

Salt Lake City Area
Advanced Awareness Counseling
http://www.advancedawarenesscounseling.com/

Washington

Seattle
Indigo Mental Health
http://www.indigomentalhealth.com/

William Soderbery, MSW
http://www.williamsoderberg.com/

Wisconsin

Forge Forward
http://forge-forward.org/in-wisconsin/referrals-and-support/therapists/

Milwaukee
Caitlin Myles, LMFT
https://www.caitlinmylestherapy.com/

Laura Liguori, PhD
http://www.amhcon.com/staff/laura-liguori.php

Organizations

Activism and Politics
National LGBTQ Campaigns & Movements
https://gendersexuality.info/campaigns/

Aging
Aging Resources
https://gendersexuality.info/aging/

Camps and Retreats
Directory of Camps for Youth, Adults, and Families
https://gendersexuality.info/camps-youth-adults-families/

Community Support & Allies
Alternate Paths
http://alternatepaths.net/

Callen Lorde Community Health Center
http://callen-lorde.org/

Clothing and Accessories Directory
https://gendersexuality.info/clothing-and-accessories/

Gender Odyssey
http://www.genderodyssey.org/

Group Psychotherapy Association of Los Angeles (GPALA)
http://www.gpala.org

K-12 Resources for Students, Teachers, Staff, and Administrators
https://gendersexuality.info/k-12-education/

LGBTQ Health
https://gendersexuality.info/health-and-medical/

Los Angeles Bi Task Force
http://labicenter.org/

Matthew Shepard Foundation
http://www.matthewshepard.org/a-horrifying-reality/

National Center for Transgender Equality
http://www.transequality.org/getting-covered-while-trans-an-open-letter-on-open-enrollment/

Online Directories of Various Resources
https://gendersexuality.info/online-directories/

The Pride Foundation
http://www.pridefoundation.org/imagine-the-possibilities/2016/06/

The Psychotherapist Association for Gender & Sexual Diversity
http://www.gaylesta.org/

Safety and Shelter Directory
https://gendersexuality.info/safety-and-shelter/

Sober Coaches of California
https://www.reachaftercare.com/sober-coaching/

Social Support and Mentorship Directory
https://gendersexuality.info/social-support-mentorship/

Suicide Prevention Directory
https://gendersexuality.info/suicide-prevention/

Susan's Place: Transgender Resources
https://www.susans.org/

Transgender Community Coalition
http://transcc.org/

Trans Narratives
http://www.transnarratives.org/index.html

YOGAY TRANS & QUEER RETREATS
http://www.yogay.net/

Conferences
The E.D.G.Y. Conference
http://www.edgyconference.com/

Eros, Embodiment & Gender: Transgender and Gender Non-Conforming Sexualities
https://www.brownpapertickets.com/event/2570826

Finding Freedom LGBTQ Symposium
https://www.michaelshouse.com/finding-freedom-lgbtq-symposium/

Gender Infinity Conference
http://genderinfinity.org/

The Transgender Training Institute, LLC
http://www.transgendertraininginstitute.com/

Eating Disorder Resources
Marcella Raimondo, PhD, MPH
http://www.marcellaedtraining.com

trans folx fighting eating disorders (TFF-ED)
http://www.transfolxfightingeds.org/

Family of LGBTQ Support
Accord Alliance
http://www.accordalliance.org/

Colage (Children of LGBTQ Support)
http://www.colage.org/

Family Equality Council: Parent Groups and
Community Resources
http://www.familyequality.org/get_involved/parent_groups/

Gay with Kids
https://gayswithkids.com/

Group for Partners of TGNC People
https://www.smore.com/rbyd2-group-for-partners-of-tgnc-people/

How Do I Tell My Kids I Have HIV?
https://www.hivplusmag.com/just-diagnosed/2016/5/05/how-do-i-tell-my-kids-i-have-hiv/

LGBTQ 101 and Beyond
https://gendersexuality.info/lgbtq-101-beyond/

Love Has No Labels
http://lovehasnolabels.com/

Parents, Family & Friends of Lesbians & Gays
https://www.pflag.org/

Transforming Family
https://www.transformingfamily.org/

TranSupport Groups at the LGBTQ Community
Center
http://www.phoenixcenterspringfield.org/transsupport-group/

Kids

Article: "Cross-Sex Hormones and Metabolic
Parameters in Adolescents with Gender Dysphoria"
https://www.ncbi.nlm.nih.gov/m/pubmed/28557738/?i=2&from=cross+sex+hormones+adolescents/

Article: "Transgender Kids Could Get Hormone
Therapy at Earlier Ages"
http://www.nbcbayarea.com/investigations/Transgender-Kids-Eligible-for-Earlier-Medical-Intervention-Under-New-Guidelines-423082734.html/

Legal & Financial Support

Financial Help
https://gendersexuality.info/financial-help/

M. Katine & J. Nechman, Attorneys at Law
https://www.lawkn.com/

Lambda Legal
https://www.lambdalegal.org/publications/xfs_kn
ow-your-rights-lgbtq-and-hiv-youth-in-foster-care/

Legal Support
https://gendersexuality.info/legal-support/

Transgender Law Center
https://transgenderlawcenter.org/archives/12193/

Transgender Law Center's Equality Map
https://transgenderlawcenter.org/equalitymap/

LGBTQ Specific Education

Asexuality
https://gendersexuality.info/collection/asexuality/

Medical Resources

The Body: The Complete HIV/AIDS Resource
http://www.thebody.com/index.html?ic=3002

Community Healthcare Network
http://www.chnnyc.org/

Health and Medical
https://gendersexuality.info/health-and-medical/

Institute for Contemporary Psychotherapy:
Psychotherapy Center for Gender & Sexuality
http://icpnyc.org/pcgs/

Metamorphosis Medical Center
http://www.metamedcenter.com/

MetroHealth Pride Clinic
http://www.metrohealth.org/prideclinic/

National LGBT Health Education Center
http://www.lgbthealtheducation.org/

Sexual Health Alliance
https://sexualhealthalliance.com/

Transgender Health Care Coverage Options
https://www.cheatsheet.com/personal-
finance/these-insurers-offer-transgender-health-
care-coverage.html/2/

Trans Pop: US Transgender Population Health
Survey
http://www.transpop.org/

Polyamory Resources
Book: *The Ethical Slut*
ISBN 978-1587613371
Celestial Arts, 2009

Book: *Opening Up: A Guide to Creating and
Sustaining Open Relationships*
by Tristan Taormino
ISBN 978-1573442954
Cleis Press, 2008

More than Two
https://www.morethantwo.com/

Multiamory Podcast
https://www.multiamory.com/podcast-summary/

Polyamory Weekly
http://polyweekly.com/

SoloPoly
https://solopoly.net/

Religious Support

Believe Out Loud
http://www.believeoutloud.com/

Family Acceptance Project
https://familyproject.sfsu.edu/

Jesus In Love Blog
http://jesusinlove.blogspot.com/

Keshet Online
https://www.keshetonline.org/about/

Religion and Spirituality
https://gendersexuality.info/religion-and-spirituality/

Soul Force
http://www.soulforce.org/

Trans Friendly Bible
https://www.facebook.com/TransFriendlyBible/?ref=bookmarks/

Support for Medical, Mental Health, and Education Professionals Serving the LGBTQIA Communities

Article: "Endocrine Treatment of Transsexual Persons: An Endocrine Society Clinical Practice Guideline"
https://press.endocrine.org/doi/full/10.1210/jc.2009-0345

Association for Lesbian, Gay, Bisexual, and Transgender Issues in Counseling
http://www.algbtic.org

California Association of Marriage and Family Therapists (CAMFT)
http://www.camft.org

Gay & Lesbian Medical Association: Health Professionals Advancing LGBT Equality
http://glma.org/

Get Down to Business Consulting
http://www.getdowntobusinessconsulting.com/

HeadCase: Call for Clinical Contributions
https://headcaseanthology.wordpress.com/2016/02/02/call-for-clinical-contributions/

Jobs and Careers
https://gendersexuality.info/jobs-and-careers/

LA Gender Center
http://lagendercenter.com/

Lesbian & Gay Psychiatric Association
http://lagpa.org/directory/

The LGBT Culture Competency Toolkit
http://www.lgbtcultcomp.org/

State of California & National Transgender
Resource Guide: A Partial Listing of Programs,
Faith Communities & Health Care Services
http://www.acphd.org/media/269820/transgender
_resource_guide.pdf

30+ Examples of Cisgender Privilege
http://itspronouncedmetrosexual.com/2011/11/lis
t-of-cisgender-privileges/

TIGRIS: Training Institute for Gender Relationships,
Identity & Sexuality
http://tigrisinstitute.com/home-study-learning

World Professional Association for Transgender
Health
http://www.wpath.org/

World Psychiatric Association: WPA Position
Statement on Gender Identity and Same-Sex
Orientation, Attraction, and Behaviours
http://www.wpanet.org/detail.php?section_id=7&
content_id=1807/

University Programs

Annette Caldwell Simmons School of Education &
Human Development Southern Methodist
University
https://www.smu.edu/StudentAffairs/WomenandL
GBTCenter/Programs/

Directory of College and Higher Education, Student Organizations, and Scholarships
https://gendersexuality.info/college-higher-education/

Lewis & Clark Graduate School
https://graduate.lclark.edu/live/events/129152-transgender-a-decolonizing-framework-for/

The Ohio State University: Transgender Primary Care Clinic
https://medicine.osu.edu/students/diversity/pages/index.aspx/

San Francisco State University Family Acceptance Project
http://familyproject.sfsu.edu/

Youth

Article: "Cross-Sex Hormones for Transgender Youth"
https://darlenetandogenderblog.com/2013/05/21/cross-sex-hormones-for-transgender-youth/

Article: "How Do You Develop Identity?"
http://www.transyouthchannel.org/blog/how-do-you-develop-identity/

Article: "Swimming as a Trans Guy"
http://theartoftransliness.com/post/25224106288/swimming-as-a-trans-guy/

Brave Trails
http://www.bravetrails.org/

Gender Spectrum
https://www.genderspectrum.org/

GLBT Hotline: Trans Teens
http://www.glbthotline.org/transteens.html/

Human Rights Campaign: Youth Report
http://www.hrc.org/youth-report/

Swimwear Dapper Boi
http://dapperboi.com/

Swimwear Outer Play
http://outplaywear.com/

Trans Student Education Resources
http://www.transstudent.org/asterisk/

The Trevor Project
https://www.thetrevorproject.org/get-help-now/

Trevor Space: Social Networking for LGBTQ Youth
https://www.trevorspace.org/

Books, Podcasts, & Media

Blogs

Darlene Tando Gender Blog
https://darlenetandogenderblog.com

Journalism, News, and Blogs
https://gendersexuality.info/journalism-news-blogs

Books

Below the Belt: Genital Talk by Men of Trans Experience
by Dr. Trystan Theosophus Cotton
ISBN 978-0986084454
Transgress Press, 2016

the GENDER book
by Mel Reiff Hill, Jay Mays, and Robin Mack
ISBN 978-0991338009
Marshall House Press, 2014
http://www.thegenderbook.com/

Helping Your Transgender Teen: A Guide for Parents
by Irwin Krieger
ISBN 978-0692012291
Genderwise Press, 2011

Looking Queer: Body Image and Identity in Lesbian, Bisexual, Gay, and Transgender Communities
by Dawn Atkins
ISBN 978-1560239314
Haworth, 1998

My Gender Workbook: How to Become a Real Man, a Real Woman, the Real You, or Something Else Entirely
by Kate Bornstein
ASIN B006P1WYJ8
Routledge, 1998

Storytelling Resources
https://gendersexuality.info/storytelling/

Trans Bodies, Trans Selves: A Resource for the Transgender Community
by Laura Erickson-Schroth
ISBN 978-0199325351
Oxford University Press, 2014

Transgender Emergence: Therapeutic Guidelines for Working With Gender-Variant People and Their Families
by Arlene Istar Lev
ISBN 978-0789021175
The Howorth Clinical Practice Press, 2004

Transgender Parents: The Ultimate Guide for Teens with Transitioning Parents
by Dr. Wendy O'Connor
ASIN B00U85SJR8
Amazon Digital Services LLC, 2015

The Transgender Teen: A Handbook for Parents and Professionals Supporting Transgender and Non-Binary Teens
by Stephanie A. Brill and Lisa Kenney
ISBN 978-1627781749
Cleis Press, 2016

Trans Sexual Violence Survivors: A Self-Help Guide to Healing and Understanding
by Michael Munson and Loree Cook-Daniels
http://forge-forward.org/2015/09/24/trans-sa-survivors-self-help-guide/

VICTIMPROOF: The Student's Guide to End Bullying
by Tom Thelen
ISBN 978-1499613711
CreateSpace Independent Publishing Platform, 2013

"You're in the Wrong Bathroom!": And 20 Other Myths and Misconceptions About Transgender and Gender-Nonconforming People
by Laura Erickson-Schroth and Laura A. Jacobs
ISBN 978-0807033890
Beacon Press, 2017

Children's Books

Be Who You Are
by Todd Parr
ISBN 978-0-316-26523-2
Little, Brown Books for Young Readers, 2016

Morris Micklewhite and the Tangerine Dress
by Christine Baldacchino and Isabelle Malenfant
ISBN 978-1554983476
Groundwood Books, 2014

Stacey's Not a Girl
by Colt Keo-Meier, Jesse Yang, and Nine Lam
ASIN B074XLLHPG
Amazon Digital Services LLC, 2017

When Kayla Was Kyle
by Amy Fabrikant and Jennifer Levine
ISBN 978-1612861548
Avid Readers Publishing Group, 2013

Podcasts

Episode: "How Parents Support their Teens Discovering their Gender Identity"
http://nicolecburgess.com/podcast/ep-37-parents-support-teen-discovering-gender-identity/

Family Confidential Podcast
http://familyconfidential.com/fcv059-parenting-lgbt-youth-susan-berland/

Gender Mom Podcast
https://gendermom.wordpress.com/

LesBe Real Radio
http://www.lesberealradio.com/

Transition Transmission Podcast
http://transitiontransmission.com/post/13028316
2607/welcome-to-the-3-year-celebration-of-
transition/

Professional Journals

Transgender Health by Mary Ann Liebert Inc.
Publishers
http://online.liebertpub.com/doi/full/10.1089/trgh
.2015.0008

Videos

"Ask Dr. Nandi: Transgender" TV Show
https://askdrnandi.com/transgender-2/

"ATTN: Transgender Shouldn't Be Afraid to Go to
the Doctor"
https://www.facebook.com/attn/videos/10626948
87099303/

Delene Van Dyk, Psychosexual Educator
https://www.youtube.com/channel/UC43qQYsXG
Q3T_S06G688_uw/

"Gay Man Asks his Parents to Come to his Wedding
on National TV"
https://www.facebook.com/pinknews/videos/101
55041976666518/

"Last Men Standing" documentary
http://projects.sfchronicle.com/2016/living-with-aids/documentary/

"The March of Marriage Equality"
https://www.youtube.com/watch?v=i2crZ4_xgKg/

PBS Documentary: "Growing Up Trans"
http://www.pbs.org/video/frontline-growing-up-trans/

"Queering Yoga: A Documentary by Ewan Duarte"
https://www.indiegogo.com/projects/queering-yoga-a-documentary-by-ewan-duarte#/

"7 Questions Answered About Transgender People"
http://abcnews.go.com/health/questions-answered-transgender-people/story?id=30570113/

"She Was the Man of My Dreams"
https://shewasthemanofmydreams.wordpress.com/

Stand With Trans playlist
https://www.youtube.com/channel/UCPPdxTT9UT-oMEos68Towpg/

TED Talk with Andrew Solomon: "How the Worst Moments in our Lives Make Us Who We Are"
http://www.ted.com/talks/andrew_solomon_how_the_worst_moments_in_our_lives_make_us_who_we_are/

TEDxBoulder with Ash Beckham: "Coming Out of Your Closet"
https://www.youtube.com/watch?v=kSR4xuU07sc

TEDxYouth@SanDiego with Eli Green: "A Toolkit for Becoming a Transgender Ally"
https://www.youtube.com/watch?v=Of-DG31_Z4w

"This Is What Nonbinary People Want You to Know"
https://www.facebook.com/buzzfeedlgbt/videos/1072745976185920/

"TRANSform WA: Meghan & Maya"
https://www.youtube.com/watch?v=q6aDOeGs9s8

"Transgender Bullying: A National Epidemic" Webinar
http://nobullying.com/transgender-bullying/

"Zanderology 101"
Available on Amazon at
https://www.amazon.com/zanderology-zander-keig/dp/b01fv0xioi/

Workbooks

The Gay and Lesbian Psychotherapy Treatment Planner
by J. M. Evosevich and Michael Avriette
ISBN 978-0471350804
Wiley, 1999

The Gender Quest Workbook: A Guide for Teens and Young Adults Exploring Gender Identity
by Rylan Jay Testa PhD; Deborah Coolhart PhD, LMFT; Jayme Peta MA, MS; Ryan K Sallans MA; and Arlene Istar Lev LCSW-R, CASAC
ISBN 978-1626252974
New Harbinger Publications, 2015

My New Gender Workbook: A Step-by-Step Guide to Achieving World Peace Through Gender Anarchy and Sex Positivity
by Kate Bornstein
ISBN 978-0415538657
Routledge, 2013

Transgender Emergence: Therapeutic Guidelines for Working With Gender-Variant People and Their Families
by Arlene Istar Lev
ISBN 978-0789021175
The Howorth Clinical Practice Press, 2004

$20 Superpack: Deconstruct Gender
by Annie Danger, Alix Kemp, Super Pack!, Helen Wildfell and Robert Wildwood
https://microcosmpublishing.com/catalog/other/6455/
Microcosm Publishing

News Articles

Allies & Families

"11 Ways To Be A Trans* Ally, According To Transgender People Themselves"
Bustle, 2015
https://www.bustle.com/articles/76762-11-ways-to-be-a-trans-ally-according-to-transgender-people-themselves/

"8 Gender Neutral Birth Terms"
Tynanrhea.com, 2017
https://www.tynanrhea.com/single-post/2017/02/13/8-gender-neutral-birth-terms-and-how-to-use-them/

"5 Accidentally Transphobic Phrases Allies Use — And What to Say Instead"
Mashable, 2015
https://mashable.com/2015/10/18/transgender-ally-words/#hVj6DWZ3csqF/

"5 Things CIS People Can Actually Do For Trans People (Now That You Care About Us)"
The (Trans)cendental Tourist, 2015
https://thetranscendentaltourist.wordpress.com/2015/06/02/5-things-cis-people-can-actually-do-for-trans-people-now-that-you-care-about-us/

"Gay & Lesbian Non Bio Parents"
Therapy4LGBT.com, n.d.
http://www.therapy4lgbt.com/non-bio-parent/

"Is Your Trans Allyship Half-Baked? Here Are 6 Mistakes That Trans Allies Are Still Making"
Everyday Feminism, 2015
https://everydayfeminism.com/2015/06/6-common-mistakes-trans-allies/

"It's Time for Trans Allies to Drop 'Identity' and Just Start Saying 'Gender'"
The New Civil Rights Movement, 2016
http://www.thenewcivilrightsmovement.com/rjmedwed/the_problem_with_gender_identity

"The Moment Daughter Learns That Daddy Is Transgender"
eBaum's World, 2016
http://www.ebaumsworld.com/videos/adorable-moment-daughter-learns-that-daddy-is-transgender/84976303/

"My Two Dads: Gay Fathers Have Much to Celebrate"
NBC News, 2016
https://www.nbcnews.com/feature/nbc-out/gay-father-s-day-n593256/

"People with Trans Parents"
Colage, n.d.
http://www.colage.org/resources/people-with-trans-parents/

"Supporting Trans* and Gender Expansive Clients and their Families"
Ackerman Institute for the Family, n.d.
http://www.ackerman.org/supporting-trans-and-gender-expansive-clients-and-their-families/

"13 Trans Latinx Activists Who Are Changing the World"
Pride.com, 2015
https://www.pride.com/transgender/2015/7/02/11-trans-latinx-activists-who-are-changing-world/

Current Events

"'All-Gender' Bathroom Bill Heads to Gov. Jerry Brown"
The Sacramento Bee, 2016
http://www.sacbee.com/news/politics-government/capitol-alert/article97270172.html/

"Anti-LGBT 'Study' Continues Long, Dark Legacy of Right-Wing Junk Science"
The New Civil Rights Movement, 2016
http://www.thenewcivilrightsmovement.com/claude_summers/pseudoscience_and_the_pursuit_of_equality/

"California, Restaurant Group to Partner in Nation's First Largescale Transgender Jobs Program"
Southern California Public Radio, 2016
http://www.scpr.org/programs/take-two/2016/09/12/51879/trans-people-will-staff-restaurants-in-new-jobs-pr/

"Council Takes on 'Conversion Therapy'"
The Daily Iowan, 2017
http://daily-iowan.com/2017/02/08/council-takes-on-conversion-therapy/

"Elite Bodybuilder Matt 'Kroc' Kroczaleski Transitions To Janae Marie Kroc"
HNGN, 2017
http://www.hngn.com/articles/113225/20150727/elite-bodybuilder-matt-kroc-kroczaleski-transitions-to-janae-marie-kroc.htm/

"Facebook Recommended that This Psychiatrist's Patients Friend Each Other"
Fusion, 2016
https://fusion.tv/story/339018/facebook-psychiatrist-privacy-problems/?utm_source=facebook&utm_medium=partner&utm_campaign=beingliberal/

"First Openly Transgender Recruit Signs Military Service Contract"
Military Times, 2018
https://www.militarytimes.com/news/your-military/2018/02/26/dod-first-openly-transgender-recruit-has-signed-contract/?utm_source=clavis/

"Gay Conversion Could Be Banned in Seattle"
KUOW, 2017
http://kuow.org/post/gay-conversion-therapy-could-be-banned-seattle

"'He Paid a Dear Price for It': The 19th-Century Ordeal of One of America's First Transgender Men"
The Washington Post, 2016
https://www.washingtonpost.com/news/morning-mix/wp/2016/09/08/he-paid-a-dear-price-for-it-the-19th-century-story-of-one-of-americas-first-transgender-men/?utm_term=.bc43b9a47cb6/

"'I Felt Like I Belonged There': Transgender Cub Scout Breaks Barrier"
The New York Times, 2017
https://www.nytimes.com/2017/02/09/nyregion/transgender-boy-scouts.html?smid=fb-share&_r=0/

"Is God Transgender?"
The New York Times, 2016
https://www.nytimes.com/2016/08/13/opinion/is-god-transgender.html?_r=0/

"London Drops Everything to Remember Orlando Victims"
Advocate, 2016
https://www.advocate.com/world/2016/6/13/london-drops-everything-remember-orlando-victims/

"Los Angeles LGBT Center Is Vandalized with Anti-LGBT Slurs"
Towleroad, 2017
http://www.towleroad.com/2017/02/lgbt-center/

"Mean Girls, Caitlyn Jenner and the Responsibility of Being a Trans Ally"
Huffington Post, 2015
https://www.huffingtonpost.com/adam-hunt/mean-girls-caitlyn-jenner_b_7883552.html/

"The New App for the Gender Variant and Queer Community"
BUST.com, n.d.
http://bust.com/living/16680-gendr.html/

"Navy to Name Ship After Gay Rights Activist Harvey Milk"
USNI News, 2016
https://news.usni.org/2016/07/28/navy-name-ship-gay-rights-activist-harvey-milk?mc_cid=6765950f0a&mc_eid=c6a190fdde/

"Obama To Name First National Monument Honoring LGBT History"
Logo.Newnownext, 2016
http://www.newnownext.com/obama-to-name-first-national-monument-honoring-lgbt-history/05/2016/?xrs=synd_facebook_logo/

"President Obama Recognizes Transgender Mothers"
Out in Perth, 2016
https://www.outinperth.com/president-obama-recognises-transgender-mothers/?fb_action_ids=951487011638263&fb_action_types=og.likes&fb_ref=.vy_arqevqsu.like/

"Queer Poetics: How to Make Love to A Trans Person"
Wild Gender, n.d.
http://wildgender.com/queer-poetics-how-to-make-love-to-a-trans-person/2401/

"Restrooms Unite Conservative Family Policy Alliance and Feminist Activists"
Colorado Politics, 2017
https://coloradopolitics.com/family-policy-transgender-restroom/

"Target to Install Gender-Neutral Bathrooms in All of Its Stores"
Advocate, 2016
https://www.advocate.com/transgender/2016/8/18/target-install-gender-neutral-bathrooms-all-its-stores/

"Texas Bill Would Allow 'Ex-Gay' Therapists, Others Who Harm LGBT People to Keep Licenses"
Towleroad, 2017
http://www.towleroad.com/2017/02/ex-gay/?utm_content=buffer482df&utm_medium=social&utm_source=facebook.com&utm_campaign=buffer/

"These Beautiful Photographs Explore The Wide Spectrum Of Gender Identity"
Huffington Post, 2016
https://www.huffingtonpost.com/entry/spectrum-of-gender-identity_us_57278077e4b0b49df6abd4c5?jpv1zb0kzqvwa02j4i/

"These New NYC Subway Ads Will Promote Transgender People's Right To Use Restrooms"
Huffington Post, 2016
https://www.buzzfeed.com/dominicholden/these-new-subway-ads-will-promote-transgender-peoples-right?utm_term=.pbzwzDzybr#.iaBO9M9q41

"This Beautiful Photo Series Encourages Employers To Hire More Trans People"
Buzzfeed, 2016
https://www.buzzfeed.com/meredithtalusan/this-inspiring-hiretrans-photo-series-celebrates-trans-peopl?utm_term=.hl6oJaJVz8&bftw=lgbt%2525252523.lhnwp1v7g#.yva8pepgjO/

"This Is How Kids Reacted to Before and After Photos of Caitlyn Jenner"
The Gaily Grind, 2015
https://thegailygrind.com/2015/06/09/this-is-how-kids-reacted-to-before-and-after-photos-of-caitlyn-jenner/

"This New Discovery About Bisexual Teen Girls Is Troubling"
TeenVogue, 2016
https://www.teenvogue.com/story/bisexual-teen-girls-depression-suicide-ideation-young-women/

"This Photo Project Is Redefining What It Means to Be African and LGBTQ"
Huffington Post, 2016
https://www.huffingtonpost.com/jaimee-a-swift/this-photo-project-african-lgbtq_b_9775092.html?utm_hp_ref=queer-voices&ir=queer+voices/

"Transgender Teen Jazz Jennings: My Family's Unconditional Love Allowed Me to Love Myself"
On Top, 2016
http://www.ontopmag.com/article/22228/Transgender_Teen_Jazz_Jennings_My_Familys_Unconditional_Love_Allowed_Me_To_Love_Myself/

"The Truth about the Massive New Study That Has Captivated Anti-LGBT Groups"
Think Progress, 2016
https://thinkprogress.org/about-that-not-born-this-way-study-b3e07d0354f5/

"24 Transgender People in History"
Weird History by Ranker
https://www.ranker.com/list/transgender-people-in-history/devon-ashby?var=4&utm_expid=16418821-201.eeizkbszs3o1rzibcocrjg.1&format=slideshow&page=1&utm_referrer=https://www.facebook.com

"UCF to Offer Course on Gender Identity"
Watermark Online, 2016
http://www.watermarkonline.com/2016/07/20/ucf-to-offer-course-on-gender-identity/

International News

"French Vogue Makes History With First Transgender Cover Model"
Huffington Post, 2017
https://www.huffingtonpost.com/entry/french-vogue-paris-valentina-sampaio-transgender-cover-model_us_58a2ce01e4b094a129ee7508/

"London Drops Everything to Remember Orlando Victims"
Advocate, 2016
https://www.advocate.com/world/2016/6/13/london-drops-everything-remember-orlando-victims/

"This Summer Camp Is Providing A Place For Trans Kids To Simply Be Themselves"
Buzzfeed, 2016
https://www.buzzfeed.com/skarlan/this-summer-camp-is-providing-a-place-for-trans-kids-to-simp?utm_term=.lgeG565Vk3#.pwQ0dmdGwe/

"What Makes These Dominican Children Grow Penises at Puberty?"
Mental Floss, 2015
http://mentalfloss.com/article/68982/what-makes-these-dominican-children-grow-penises-puberty/

Legal

"California Becomes First State to Ban Gay, Trans 'Panic' Defenses"
Advocate, 2014
https://www.advocate.com/crime/2014/09/29/california-becomes-first-state-ban-gay-trans-panic-defenses/

"Gay Conversion Therapy Ban Upheld by 9th Circ."
Courthouse News, 2016
https://www.courthousenews.com/gay-conversion-therapy-ban-upheld-by-9th-circ/

Gloucester County School Board v. G.G.
SCOTUSblog, 2017
http://www.scotusblog.com/case-files/cases/gloucester-county-school-board-v-g-g/

"Hawaii Bill Allowing Transgender People to Amend Birth Certificates Signed into Law"
Human Rights Campaign, 2015
http://www.hrc.org/blog/hawaii-bill-allowing-transgender-people-to-amend-birth-certificates-signed/

"John Oliver Shows Just How Far We Have To Go On Transgender Rights"
Huffington Post, 2015
https://www.huffingtonpost.com/2015/06/29/john-oliver-transgender-rights_n_7686976.html/

"Mississippi Governor Signs Law Allowing Businesses to Refuse Service to Gay People"
Washington Post, 2016
https://www.washingtonpost.com/news/post-nation/wp/2016/04/05/mississippi-governor-signs-law-allowing-business-to-refuse-service-to-gay-people/?utm_term=.07993eea4363/

"Senate panel unanimously approves ban on conversion therapy"
NM Political Report, 2017
http://nmpoliticalreport.com/149923/senate-panel-unanimously-approves-ban-on-conversion-therapy/

"Toledo City Council Unanimously Approved a Ban on Conversion Therapy"
The Blade, 2017
http://www.toledoblade.com/politics/2017/02/07/toledo-city-council-unanimously-approves-ban-on-conversion-therapy-also-makes-gender-identity-protected-class.html/

"UPDATING: US Dept. Of Justice Says HB2 Violates Federal Civil Rights Act, Demands Implementation End"
New Civil Rights Movement, 2016
http://www.thenewcivilrightsmovement.com/davidbadash/breaking_us_dept_of_justice_says_hb2_violates_federal_civil_rights_act_demands_implementation_end/

"Why Gay Rights and Trans Rights Should Be Separated"
Huffington Post, 2014
https://www.huffingtonpost.com/tyler-curry/gay-rights-and-trans-rights_b_4763380.html/

Medical

"The Difference Between Dysphoria and Negative Body Image"
AmyDentata.com, 2012
http://amydentata.com/2012/03/06/the-difference-between-dysphoria-and-negative-body-image/

"8 Myths About Transgender Men's Genital Reconstructions"
Huffington Post, 2014
https://www.huffingtonpost.com/mitch-kellaway/8-myths-about-transgender-mens-genital-reconstructions_b_4510196.html/

"Hormone Therapy is Lifesaving — But Why is No One Studying Its Long-Term Effects?"
Out, 2016
https://www.out.com/out-exclusives/2016/9/20/hormone-therapy-lifesaving-why-no-one-studying-its-long-term-effects/

"How a Tiny City in New York Became a Beacon for Transgender Healthcare"
The Guardian, 2016
https://www.theguardian.com/society/2016/may/03/transgender-healthcare-doctor-oneonta-new-york-carolyn-wolf-gould/

"How Sexual Addiction Treatments Fail When Working with Gay and Bisexual Men"
Huffington Post, 2015
https://www.huffingtonpost.com/joe-kort-phd/how-sexual-addiction-trea_b_8683926.html/

"How to Find an Accepting Therapist"
Advocate, 2016
https://www.advocate.com/commentary/2016/4/20/how-find-accepting-therapist/

"How Trans Women Are Reclaiming Their Orgasms"
Buzzfeed, 2016
https://www.buzzfeed.com/kaichengthom/the-search-for-trans-womens-orgasms?utm_term=.urLvlVlAL9#.ger7WnWMoz/

"LGBT Aging Issues Network"
American Society on Aging, n.d.
http://www.asaging.org/lain/

"LGBT Suicide and the Trauma of Growing Up Gay"
PsychCentral, n.d.
https://psychcentral.com/lib/lgbt-suicide-and-the-trauma-of-growing-up-gay/

"Low-Income Transgender Patients in Southern California Don't Have Access to Life-Changing Surgeries"
California Health Report, 2016
http://www.calhealthreport.org/2016/09/12/low-income-transgender-patients-in-southern-california-dont-have-access-to-life-changing-surgeries/

"National Pilot Program to Train Doctors in Transgender Health"
USA Today, 2015
https://www.usatoday.com/story/news/nation/2015/06/11/training-doctors-in-transgender-health/71060642/

"Sexuality is Fluid – It's Time to Get Past 'Born This Way'"
New Scientist, 2015
https://www.newscientist.com/article/mg22730310-100-sexuality-is-fluid-its-time-to-get-past-born-this-way/

"Texas Seeks to Allow Doctors Right to Refuse Treating Transgender Patients"
Houston Press, 2016
http://www.houstonpress.com/news/texas-seeks-to-allow-doctors-right-to-refuse-treating-transgender-patients-8696654/

"Trans Folks Now Have A Safe Space To Recover From Gender Confirmation Surgery"
Huffington Post, 2016
https://www.huffingtonpost.com/entry/rhys-place-gender-confirmation-surgery_us_577fd52ce4b0c590f7e91d73?/

"Transforming The Doctor's Office To Welcome Transgender Patients"
Rhode Island Public Radio, 2015
http://ripr.org/post/transforming-doctors-office-welcome-transgender-patients/

"The Transgender Community Has a New Way to Find the Right Doctor"
The Daily Good, 2015
https://www.good.is/articles/new-app-helps-trans-people-find-trans-friendly-doctors/

"Transgender Identity Classification"
LiveScience, 2016
https://www.livescience.com/55554-transgender-identity-classification.html/

"TriCare to Cover Transgender Treatment Options"
Military.com, 2018
https://www.military.com/daily-news/2016/08/21/tricare-now-covering-transgender-treatment-options.html/

"What Surgeons Need to Know About Gender
Confirmation Surgery When Providing Care for
Transgender Individuals"
The JAMA Network, 2017
https://jamanetwork.com/journals/jamasurgery/ar
ticle-abstract/2600158/

Teens & Youth

"Arin Andrews and Katie Hill, Transgender Teenage
Couple, Transition Together"
Huffington Post, 2013
https://www.huffingtonpost.com/2013/07/23/tran
sgender-teenage-couple-arin-andrews-katie-
hill_n_3639220.html/

"Chicago schools say transgender kids should use
bathrooms matching identity"
USA Today, 2016
https://www.usatoday.com/story/news/2016/05/0
3/chicago-schools-say-transgender-kids-should-
use-bathrooms-matching-identity/83880078/

"City of Miami Looks to Ban Conversion Therapy
for Gay Minors"
Miami New Times, 2016
http://www.miaminewtimes.com/news/city-of-
miami-looks-to-ban-conversion-therapy-for-gay-
minors-8753836/

"15 Of the 'Absolute Worst' College Campuses for LGBTQ Youth, Via Campus Pride"
Huffington Post, 2016
https://www.huffingtonpost.com/entry/2016-college-shame-list_us_57c45ccee4b09cd22d919071?/

"From A to T: Advice for Trans* and Gender Nonconforming Teens, Adolescents, Families, and Allies! Home for the Holidays Edition"
Huffington Post, 2015
https://www.huffingtonpost.com/laura-a-jacobs-lcswr/from-a-to-t-advice-for-tr_b_8817876.html/

"New CHLA Study Uncovers Baseline Characteristics of Transyouth Seeking Care for Gender Dysphoria"
News Medical: Life Sciences, 2015
http://www.news-medical.net/news/20150722/new-chla-study-uncovers-baseline-characteristics-of-transyouth-seeking-care-for-gender-dysphoria.aspx/

"An Open Letter to Justice, the Tween Girls' Clothing Store"
Huffington Post, 2016
https://www.huffingtonpost.com/entry/an-open-letter-to-the-tween-girls-clothing-store-justice_us_57d54f2de4b0eb9a57b7acf4?ir=good+news&/

"Puberty Blockers May Improve the Mental Health of Transgender Adolescents"
California Healthline, 2016
https://californiahealthline.org/news/puberty-blockers-may-improve-the-mental-health-of-transgender-adolescents/

"Seattle Children's to open Gender Clinic in October"
K5 News, 2016
http://www.king5.com/article/news/health/seattle-childrens-to-open-gender-clinic-in-october/315284453/

"Transgender at School: As More Teachers Come Out, Districts Struggle to Put Policy into Practice"
Oregon Live, 2016
http://www.oregonlive.com/portland/index.ssf/2015/09/transgender_teachers_oregon.html/

"A Transgender 9-year-old Tells her Story"
L.A. Times, 2016
http://www.latimes.com/local/education/la-me-0516-transgender-student-20160513-snap-htmlstory.html/

"Transgender Student Accuses School of 'Stigmatizing' Treatment"
CNN, 2016
https://www.cnn.com/2016/07/20/us/wisconsin-transgender-student-lawsuit/index.html/

"Transgender Student Tells East Penn School
Board: Thank You for Welcoming Me"
The Morning Post, 2016
http://www.mcall.com/news/local/eastpenn/mc-
east-penn-trangender-conversation-bathroom-
locker-room-20160913-story.html/

"When Teenage Girls Find Out They're Genetically
Male"
Broadly, 2015
https://broadly.vice.com/en_us/article/4xkedq/wh
en-teenage-girls-find-out-theyre-genetically-male/

"With School's Blessing, This Valedictorian Comes
Out as Gay During Graduation Speech"
LGBTQ Nation, 2015
https://www.lgbtqnation.com/2015/06/with-
schools-blessing-this-valedictorian-comes-out-as-
gay-during-graduation-speech/

Trans Partners

"Dating Is More than Waiting: Make Your Own
Opportunities"
GoodTherapy.org, 2016
https://www.goodtherapy.org/blog/dating-is-
more-than-waiting-make-your-own-opportunities-
0826164/

"Stop Shaming Partners of Trans People"
Huffington Post, 2015
http://www.huffingtonpost.com/thomas-matt/stop-shaming-partners-of-trans-people_b_7900302.html/

"Transgender at War and In Love"
The New York Times, 2015
https://www.nytimes.com/video/opinion/100000003720527/transgender-at-war-and-in-love.html/

"The Transgender Dating Dilemma"
Buzzfeed, 2015
https://www.buzzfeed.com/raquelwillis/the-transgender-dating-dilemma?utm_term=.dtBd3r3LAN#.yx7OR9R0jv/

Trans Seniors

"Providing Competent and Affirming Services for Transgender and Gender Nonconforming Older Adults"
Taylor & Francis Online, 2016
https://www.tandfonline.com/doi/full/10.1080/07317115.2016.1203383/

Uncategorized

"Electrolysis vs. Laser Hair Removal"
LiveAbout, 2017
https://www.liveabout.com/electrolysis-versus-laser-hair-removal-1716760/

"For Transgender Men, Clothing Can Be Self-Determination"
Mic, 2016
https://mic.com/articles/139420/for-transgender-men-clothing-can-be-self-determination#.a0JdhJjnT/

"The Future is Bright for Bisexual People, Despite Our Current Challenges"
Huffington Post, 2016
https://www.huffingtonpost.com/neil-endicott/the-future-is-bright-for-_b_8749242.html?ir=gay+voices&/

"The Genderbread Person 2.0"
It's Pronounced 'Metrosexual', n.d.
http://itspronouncedmetrosexual.com/2012/03/the-genderbread-person-v2-0/

"Growing Old Gracefully: The Transgender Experience"
TransHealth, 2012
http://www.trans-health.com/2012/growing-old-gracefully/

"How Do You Know You're a Woman?"
The Cut, 2015
https://www.thecut.com/2015/06/how-do-you-know-youre-a-woman.html?om_rid=aawzif&om_mid=_bvezccb9cf$9ft/

"North Carolina, U.S., Square Off Over Transgender Rights"
CNN: Politics, 2016
https://www.cnn.com/2016/05/09/politics/north-carolina-hb2-justice-department-deadline/index.html/

"Op-Ed: Violence Against Trans Men Will Lessen If We Address Trans Women's Oppression"
Advocate, 2015
https://www.advocate.com/commentary/2015/07/17/op-ed-violence-against-trans-men-will-lessen-if-we-address-trans-womens-oppres?team=social/

The Pride LA Newspaper
https://thepridela.com/

"The Remarkable Journey From Identical Twins To Brother And Sister"
Huffington Post, 2015
https://www.huffingtonpost.com/entry/nicole-maines-book_us_5624f17be4b02f6a900ce129/

"Separate But Equal: Transgender Disclosure"
Huffington Post, 2015
https://www.huffingtonpost.com/zoe-dolan/separate-but-equal-transgender-disclosure_b_7889524.html/

"Trans Artists Made These Stunning Posters for Trans Day of Remembrance"
Buzzfeed, 2015
https://www.buzzfeed.com/meredithtalusan/stunning-posters-aim-to-transform?utm_term=.xsL4NjNe2p#.fjreQXQRDN/

"This Trans Guy Wrote a Letter to the Little Girl He Once Was to Say Sorry"
Buzzfeed, 2015
https://www.buzzfeed.com/patrickstrudwick/from-ethan-to-emily?bffblgbt&utm_term=.ii6kZpZg7B#.vnq5GBGoAq/

"The Trans Movement: Is This The Transgender Community's Moment?"
Southern California Public Radio, 2015
http://www.scpr.org/programs/take-two/2015/07/29/43882/the-trans-movement-is-this-the-transgender-communi/

"Trans* Year End Reflections: The Shape of Things to Come"
Huffington Post, 2015
https://www.huffingtonpost.com/laura-a-jacobs-lcswr/trans-year-end-reflection_b_8884128.html/

"What They Don't Tell You About Being Transgender"
Everyday Feminism, 2015
https://everydayfeminism.com/2015/06/things-dont-tell-you-being-transgender/

"Why Non-Natives Appropriating 'Two-Spirit'
Hurts"
BGBD, 2016
http://www.bgdblog.org/2016/07/appropriating-
two-spirit/

"You Can Still Be Transgender If You Don't Feel
Physical Dysphoria – Here's Why"
Everyday Feminism, 2016
https://everydayfeminism.com/2016/05/transgend
er-without-dysphoria/

<h1 style="text-align:center">Bibliography</h1>

American Psychiatric Association. (1987). *Diagnostic and statistical manual of mental disorders. DSM-III-R. Prep.* Washington: American Psychiatric Association.

American Psychiatric Association. (2014a). *Diagnostic and statistical manual of mental disorders.* (5th ed.). Washington DC: American Psychiatric Association.

American Psychiatric Association. (2014b). Gender dysphoria. *Diagnostic and statistical manual of mental disorders.* (5th ed.). Washington DC: American Psychiatric Association.

Bellis, R. (2016, March 03). *Here's Everywhere In America You Can Still Get Fired For Being Gay Or Trans.* Retrieved May 28, 2018, from https://www.fastcompany.com/3057357/heres-everywhere-in-america-you-can-still-get-fired-for-

being-lgbt

Brown Boi Project. (2010). Retrieved May 28, 2018,

from http://www.brownboiproject.org/

Deutsch, M. B., MD, MPH. (n.d.a). Overview of

feminizing hormone therapy. Retrieved May 28,

2018, from

http://transhealth.ucsf.edu/trans?page=guidelines

-feminizing-therapy

Deutsch, M. B., MD, MPH. (n.d.b). Overview of

masculizing hormone therapy. Retrieved May 28,

2018, from

http://transhealth.ucsf.edu/trans?page=guidelines

-masculinizing-therapy

"Facts about suicide." The Trevor Project. (n.d.).

Retrieved May 28, 2018, from

http://www.thetrevorproject.org/pages/facts-about-suicide

Ferguson, A. S. (2014, September 26). Privilege 101: A quick and dirty guide. Retrieved May 28, 2018, from http://everydayfeminism.com/2014/09/what-is-privilege/

Guay, J., LMFT. (2016, July 22). *Affirmative therapy with transgender and gender non-conforming clients.* Lecture presented at Los Angles California Marriage & Family Therapy Association (LA-CAMFT) Networking Brunch in The Olympic Collection, Los Angeles.

Lartey, J. (2016, December 08). *The guardian.* Risk of poverty and suicide far higher among transgender people, survey finds. Retrieved May 28, 2018, from https://www.theguardian.com/society/2016/dec/0

8/transgender-survey-suicide-poverty-

unemployment-mental-health

LGBT Issues Committee of the Group for the

Advancement of Psychiatry (GAP). (2011).

Welcome. Retrieved May 28, 2018, from

http://www.aglp.org/gap/

Pan, L., & Moore, A. (2017). The Gender Unicorn.

Retrieved May 28, 2018, from

http://www.transstudent.org/gender

Singh, D.; Deogracias, J. J.; Johnson, L. L.; Bradley, S. J.;

Kibblewhite, S. J.; Owen-Anderson, A.; Peterson-

Badali, M.; Meyer-Bahlburg, H.; and Zucker, K. J.

(2010). The gender identity/gender dysphoria

questionnaire for adolescents and adults: Further

validity evidence. *Journal of Sex Research*, 47(1),

49-58. doi:10.1080/00224490902898728

Transition (2017). In *Merriam-Webster's dictionary.*

    Retrieved May 28, 2018, from

    https://www.merriam-

    webster.com/dictionary/change

University of North Carolina at Charlotte. (n.d.a). Safe

    Zone. Retrieved May 28, 2018, from

    https://safezone.uncc.edu/

University of North Carolina at Charlotte. (n.d.b).

    Theories on LGBTQ Development. Retrieved May

    28, 2018, from

    https://safezone.uncc.edu/allies/theories

World Professional Association for Transgender Health

    (WPATH). (n.d.). Retrieved May 28, 2018, from

    http://www.wpath.org/

Index

A **bold** designation indicates the page number on which a term is defined. A designation of n indicates that on the listed page, a reference is made to the end notes. Images are designated by [image] after the appropriate page number.

About the Author

Traci Lowenthal, PsyD, is a licensed clinical psychologist and owner of Creative Insights Counseling in California. In her profession, she works with many people, though much of her training, and over 13 years of experience has focused on working with and supporting the LGBTIQ community. In particular, she has worked with many people for whom society's labels failed to articulate their true identity, a calling to which she feels privileged. Traci loves being a psychologist because she is able to witness people regain hope, strength, and contentment in their lives.

Traci can be reached through her website at https://creativeinsightscounseling.com/

www.ingramcontent.com/pod-product-compliance
Lightning Source LLC
Chambersburg PA
CBHW070118260726

48658CB00001B/163